HO
& OAHU

BONNIE FRIEDMAN

EYEWITNESS TRAVEL

Left **The Waikīkī skyline** Right **Polynesian Cultural Center**

LONDON, NEW YORK,
MELBOURNE, MUNICH AND DELHI
www.dk.com

Produced by Blue Island, London
Reproduced by Colourscan, Singapore Printed and
bound by South China Printing Co. Ltd, China
Published in the United States by
DK Publishing,
375 Hudson Street, New York,
New York 10014
First American Edition, 2004
12 13 14 15 10 9 8 7 6 5 4 3 2
Reprinted with revisions 2006, 2008, 2010, 2012
Copyright 2004, 2012
© Dorling Kindersley Limited, London
A Penguin Company

A catalog record for this book is available from the
Library of Congress.
ISSN 1479-344X
ISBN: 978-0-75668-458-7

Within each Top 10 list in this book, no hierarchy of
quality or popularity is implied. All 10 are, in the
editor's opinion, of roughly equal merit.

MIX
Paper from
responsible sources
FSC
www.fsc.org   FSC™ C018179

Contents

Top 10 of Honolulu & O'ahu

Left **Waikīkī Beach** Center **Performance, Kalākaua Avenue** Right **Chinatown**

Left **Kualoa Regional Park** Right **Byodo-in Temple**

Key to abbreviations
Adm admission charge payable **Free** no admission charge

3

TOP 10 OF HONOLULU & O'AHU

Highlights of Honolulu & O'ahu

O'ahu is the most populous of the Hawaiian islands, and its conjoined hubs are the city of Honolulu and the world-famous Waikīkī Beach. The vast majority of visitors make Waikīkī their base, venturing out on day trips to take in Honolulu's many cultural attractions, Pearl Harbor, and other parts of the island. The family-friendly beaches and parks of the South Shore and Kāne'ohe District are in striking distance of Honolulu, while diehard surfers head for the North Shore. The Polynesian Cultural Center is also an easy day trip from the city.

Pearl Harbor
The World War II site draws 1.5 million visitors each year, including veterans and relatives of those who died. The warship *USS Arizona* is now a memorial. *(See pp8–9.)*

Bishop Museum and Planetarium
This state museum in Honolulu offers a fascinating insight into Hawaiian culture. Its Science Garden represents the unique Hawaiian land divisions called *ahupua'a*. *(See pp10–11.)*

Māmala

Capitol District
Chinatown, the modern State Capitol, and an old mansion that was once the home of Queen Lili'uokalani are just some of the attractions of this historic district in Honolulu. *(See pp12–13.)*

'Iolani Palace
The palace was built for King Kalākaua and Queen Kapi'olani in the 19th century and was later the seat of government. It is now restored and open to the public. *(See pp14–15.)*

Chinatown
This 15-block historic district should more accurately be called Southeast Asia Town. It is home to food purveyors, farmers' markets, gift shops, *lei* stands, art galleries, and eateries. *(See pp16–17.)*

Previous pages **Statue of Kamehameha, Honolulu Capitol District**

Honolulu Academy of Arts

Arts of the Islamic and Oriental worlds are strong points of this museum, as well as 15,000 works by American and European artists. Polynesian works are displayed, too. *(See pp18–19.)*

Kalākaua Avenue 7

Kalākaua is Waikīkī's main thoroughfare, running along the ocean right up to the crater of Diamond Head. Halfway along the avenue are the "Pink Lady" and the "White Lady" – two landmark, oceanfront hotels with famous bars. *(See pp20–21.)*

South Shore 8

The South Shore of O'ahu has among its attractions several popular beaches, walking trails over Koko Head, and an underwater park at Hanauma Bay. *(See pp22–23.)*

Polynesian Cultural Center 10

On the north shore of O'ahu, this center is the place to explore the rich traditions of Polynesia, such as the pageantry and cuisines of Hawai'i, Tahiti, Tonga, and other Pacific islands. *(See pp26–27.)*

Kāne'ohe District 9

A stunning region northeast of Honolulu, Kāne'ohe has a scenic coastline, lush gardens, state parks, and a Japanese-style temple to explore. *(See pp24–25.)*

Pearl Harbor

Set in a bay where Hawaiians once harvested clams and oysters (hence the "pearl" connection), the infamous World War II site is still a key military base. The harbor's relics and memorials, which incorporate the resting place of the doomed battleship Arizona *and final berth of the historic* USS Missouri, *are visited by 1.5 million people each year. A museum of military aviation is also nearby.*

USS Arizona Memorial

🔰 Security measures are in place, and bags may have to be secured in lockers. Carry only what you need and, of course, nothing that might qualify as a weapon.

The attractions of Pearl Harbor may be too much for small children — too much waiting and walking.

• Map D5
• Visitor Center:
1 Arizona Pl.;
www.nps.gov/usar;
422 0561; 7am–5pm;
free
• USS Bowfin Submarine
Museum: 11 Arizona
Memorial Dr.;
www.bowfin.org;
8am–5pm daily; adm
$10; no children under 4
• USS Missouri:
www.ussmissouri.com;
9am–5pm daily; adm
for self-guided tours
($20 adults/$10 children),
additional fees for
special tours, such as
the Battle Stations
Tour ($45 adults/
$22 children)

Top 10 Sights

1. Battleship Row
2. USS Arizona Visitor Center
3. USS Arizona Museum
4. Historical Film
5. USS Arizona Memorial
6. USS Bowfin Park
7. USS Bowfin Submarine Museum
8. USS Missouri
9. Battle Stations Tour
10. Deck of Surrender

2 USS Arizona Visitor Center

Thousands of people pass daily through the center *(above)*, which is the gateway to the offshore memorial. Arrive early: free, timed tickets for the movie and boat ride are gone by noon on busy days. And even then, expect several hours' wait.

3 USS Arizona Museum

This collection of interpretive exhibits and artifacts is one place to visit during the time you'll inevitably spend waiting for the boat.

1 Battleship Row

The U.S. docked the workhorses of its Pacific fleet along the shore of Ford Island. Vulnerably positioned, the ships sustained the full force of the attack on the morning of December 7, 1941.

Mighty Mo (USS Missouri)

4 Historical Film

The 23-minute documentary film shown at the Visitor Center gives viewers a broad outline of the forces that led up to the Pearl Harbor attack and the main events of that fateful day.

5 USS Arizona Memorial

The stark white structure, floating above the ship that became a tomb, is a place to solemnly peruse the names of the dead inscribed on the wall *(below)*.

6 USS Bowfin Park

This park, entryway to the submarine museum, plays host to a display of weaponry, including a deadly looking Poseidon C-3 Missile *(above)* and a Japanese human torpedo.

7 USS Bowfin Submarine Museum

If the *Arizona* is representative of the attack on the U.S., the *Bowfin* helps visitors understand how the country responded. Nicknamed Pearl Harbor Avenger, SS-287 has tales to tell of wartime patrols and conditions for submariners *(below)*.

8 USS Missouri

Twenty stories high and three football fields long, this vessel has earned its nickname, Mighty Mo. Approximately half of the ship is open to visitors.

10 Deck of Surrender

A bronze floor plaque *(above)* in the teak deck on the *USS Missouri* marks where a mess table was set up for Japanese ministers to sign the Instruments of Surrender in Tokyo Harbor in 1945.

9 Battle Stations Tour

This expensive but highly recommended 90-minute tour of the *Missouri* is the most comprehensive tour available. It focuses on stories of the ship's many battles. Children must be aged 10 or over.

"A Day That Will Live in Infamy"

That was how President Roosevelt described December 7, 1941, when the Japanese made a surprise attack on Pearl Harbor. The bombers crippled U.S. military installations on O'ahu, sinking or severely damaging 18 battleships at rest in Pearl Harbor, destroying or disabling nearly 200 aircraft, and killing 2,390 officers and men. The U.S. officially entered World War II after this event.

TOP 10 Bishop Museum and Planetarium

The State Museum for Natural and Cultural History is a family-friendly center for scientific and cultural experience and study. It also hosts traveling exhibitions and is home to the Jhamandus Watumull planetarium. Almost every weekend, and on many weeknights, there are lectures, workshops, and openings. The museum also has a fascinating interactive science center.

Busts and paintings in the Picture Gallery

Main entrance

🌀 The museum's shop, Pacifica, is a wonderful gift emporium – one of the island's best. The quality of its souvenirs is excellent, and the wide-ranging book selection runs from history to science, and archaeology to anthropology.

• 1525 Bernice St., Honolulu
• Map A5
• 847 3511
• www. bishopmusem.org
• 9am–5pm Mon, Wed–Sun; closed Dec 25
• Adm $17.95, child (ages 4–12) and seniors $14.95 (discounts for local residents and military)

Top 10 Highlights

1. Polynesian Hall
2. Hawaiian Hall
3. Picture Gallery
4. Kāhili Room
5. Hawai'i Sports Hall of Fame
6. Library
7. Richard T. Mamiya Science Center
8. Castle Memorial Building
9. Joseph M. Long Gallery
10. Planetarium

1 Polynesian Hall

Two floors of the museum are devoted to Pacific cultures other than Hawai'i's. The artifacts give an insight into rituals and religion, daily life, warfare, clothing, music, and dance, and include carved figures *(below)*.

Richard T. Mamiya Science Center

2 Hawaiian Hall

The *koa*-paneled Hawaiian Hall, built in Victorian architectural style, is the heart of the museum. It is home to a vast collection of Hawaiian and Pacific area artifacts. The hall presents its stunning collections in a modern interpretation of Hawai'i's history and culture.

3 Picture Gallery

Considered the world's finest collection of 19th-century Hawaiian art, the museum's extraordinary collection of oil paintings, watercolors, rare books, and collectibles are on display here.

Kāhili Room
Beloved by the Hawaiian people, this collection honors Hawaiian royalty through portraiture and displays of royal belongings, including the fragile feather standards called *kāhili (above)*.

Entrance to main museum

To the main entrance

Hawai'i Sports Hall of Fame
This is an unusual installation *(above)* for a cultural museum, but islanders are crazy about sports, which are a primary form of community-building.

Library
This extensive library includes a database of published diaries, narratives, and memoirs, all with an emphasis on Hawai'i and Pacific culture.

Richard T. Mamiya Science Center
Interactive experiences, including erupting volcanoes and deep ocean exploration, are offered at this state-of-the-art center.

Joseph M. Long Gallery
This gallery serves as Bishop Museum's venue for showcasing contemporary Hawaiian art alongside other items from the museum's collections. This grass sculpture *(above)* is an example of some of the native Hawaiian art pieces on display.

Castle Memorial Building
Dinosaurs, robots, spiders, chocolate, and volcanoes have been the subjects of visiting exhibitions. Most are interactive and aim to pull in youngsters.

Planetarium
The exceptionally active planetarium stages interactive shows, night-viewing sessions, and the "Science on a Sphere" exhibit in the lobby *(below)*.

The Ahupua'a
Ahupua'a – the wedge-shaped units of land shown in the museum's Science Garden – were overseen by *konohiki* (governors), who funneled taxes to royalty. The *ahupua'a* encompassed various farming regions and fishing grounds in order to meet the subsistence needs of their inhabitants.

TOP 10 Capitol District

If you had but one day to spend in Honolulu, there's an argument to be made for spending it right here. Concentrated within a few misshapen blocks is a clutch of historic landmarks, a toothsome Asian marketplace, a neighborhood of fragrant lei stands, and alluring shops, galleries, and restaurants. And when it's time to sit and contemplate, there's also an ample store of shady mini-parks and cool retreats on hand.

Kawaiaha'o Church

🔵 Re-energize at Cafe Laniakea in the historic YWCA building (1040 Richards St., 536 7061), or in the café of the Hawai'i State Art Museum.

- Map J2–K3
- Museum of Art: 250 S. Hotel St.; 10am–4pm Tue–Sat; 586 0900; Free
- Ali'iolani Hale: 417 S. King St.; Mon–Fri; guided tours by appt. 539 4999
- Library: 478 S. King St.; Mon–Sat; 586 3500
- Kawaiaha'o Church: Punchbowl and King Sts.; 8:30am–4pm Mon–Fri
- Mission Houses Museum: 553 South King St.; 10am–4pm Tue–Sat; 531 0481; Adm $10

Top 10 Sights

1. Washington Place
2. Hawai'i State Capitol
3. Hawai'i State Art Museum
4. Coronation Pavilion
5. King Kamehameha Statue
6. Ali'iolani Hale
7. Hawai'i State Library
8. Mission Houses Museum
9. Kawaiaha'o Church
10. St. Andrew's Cathedral

Hawai'i State Capitol

The airy structure of 1969 is imbued with symbolic references to Hawai'i. Pools represent the sea, the columns reach up like tall trees, and the conical roofline recalls the volcanoes that formed these islands. In front of the building is a statue of Queen Lili'uokalani *(left)*.

Hawai'i State Art Museum

In 1967, Hawai'i became the first U.S. state to have an annual budget for art purchases. But it wasn't until 2002 that the collection found its permanent home to showcase solely the work of island artists.

Washington Place

This elegant mansion has been turned into a museum for Hawai'i's last queen, Lili'uokalani, the abode's most famous resident. It is home to the current governor.

Hawai'i State Art Museum

Coronation Pavilion

On the grounds of 'Iolani Palace *(see pp14–15)* is an ornate pavilion, erected especially for the coronation of King Kalākaua and Queen Kapi'olani in 1883. The octagonal, copper-roofed structure, which is emblazoned with the Hawaiian royal seal, serves as a bandstand for the Royal Hawaiian Band. They perform free concerts at noon most Fridays and for gubernatorial inaugurations.

5 King Kamehameha Statue

During King Kamehameha Day celebrations each June *(see p36)*, the King Street statue *(left)* is decorated with thousands of flowers, strung into exuberant *lei* (garlands).

6 Ali'iōlani Hale

The "House of Heavenly Royalty" is the site of the Hawai'i Supreme Court, and it also houses the free Judiciary History Center. Here, there are exhibits and multimedia presentations on Hawai'i's legal history and landmark cases.

7 Hawai'i State Library

The Hawai'i State Library building, with its colonnaded façade and mullioned windows, is a cool oasis amid the bustle of downtown. The Pacific section is especially worth a visit, as is the attractive enclosed courtyard.

8 Mission Houses Museum

This living history museum *(above)* includes one of the earliest examples of American domestic architecture, the coral-block Chamberlain House (1830), as well as two other missionary buildings. There is an excellent gift shop.

10 St. Andrew's Cathedral

This Gothic-vaulted cathedral *(above)* took nearly 100 years to build and is the oldest Episcopal edifice in Hawai'i. It was consecrated in 1958, upon completion of the final phase of construction.

9 Kawaiaha'o Church

Built by volunteers out of 14,000 hand-cut coral blocks, "Hawai'i's Westminster" offers religious services in Hawaiian and English. Its name has a double meaning, referring to a legend about a sacred chiefess who caused water to flow here so she could bathe, and also to a Biblical reference about "living waters".

Queen Lili'uokalani

Washington House was the home of Lili'uokalani, the last queen of Hawai'i, who ruled from 1891 until she was deposed by the advocates of a Republic for Hawai'i in 1893. She was married to John Dominis, who owned Washington House, and later inherited the house from her husband's family.

TOP 10 'Iolani Palace

A National Historic Landmark, this is the only state residence of royalty in the U.S. It was built for King David Kalākaua and his queen, Kapi'olani, and was the home of his sister, Queen Lili'uokalani, until her reign ended in 1893. From 1893 to 1968 'Iolani was the seat of the Hawaiian government. Heavily restored, it includes priceless objects and gorgeous decorative touches.

Inner courtyard

Statue of King Kalākaua and palace tower

🕐 Note that under-fives are not admitted on palace tours.

• Map J3
• Corner of King and Richards streets, Capitol District, Honolulu
• Recorded info: 538 1471; tickets: 522 0832
• www.iolanipalace.org
• 9am–5pm Mon–Sat
• Adm: gallery self-guided tour $12 adults, $5 children; 90-min guided grand tour with film $20 adults, $6 children
• Shop: 8:30am–4pm Mon–Sat

Top 10 Sights

1. Gates and Coat of Arms
2. Burial Mound
3. 'Iolani Barracks
4. Central Hall and Staircase
5. Blue Room
6. Queen Lili'uokalani's Room
7. King's Suite
8. Throne Room
9. Dining Room
10. Palace Galleries

Gates and Coat of Arms

The Kauikeaouli Gate, which opens onto King Street, was the ceremonial entrance, used only on state occasions. Mounted on its bars is the Hawaiian coat of arms *(above)*, popular with islanders today in the form of medallions or amulets.

Burial Mound

Although the chiefly burials were moved to the Royal Mausoleum in Nu'uanu in 1865, this mound to one side of the palace remains an object of respect, as some bones may remain.

Palace façade

'Iolani Barracks

The diminutive but historic barracks *(below)* for the King's guard now house the palace shop, ticket office, and video theater. The shop specializes in one-of-a-kind designs based on palace ornaments, such as bookmarks derived from the ornate carving on the palace door hinges.

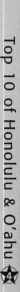

Central Hall and Staircase
This capacious and distinctive hall has doors to the front and back for light and ventilation, and is hung with royal portraits. The impressive staircase *(above)* is the work of royal advisor Walter Murray Gibson.

Blue Room
In this first-floor room, the King received guests informally. A portrait of King Louis Philippe of France dominates; the French were among several countries that considered a closer alliance with (or even a take-over of) the Hawaiian kingdom.

Queen Lili'uokalani's Room
On the second floor is the room where Lili'uokalani *(below)* was confined for eight months after the overthrow of the monarchy. She was charged with being involved in an insurrection.

King's Suite
Kalākaua slept in a state bedroom with heavy Victorian furnishings, while in the library he conducted business and played cards. One of the islands' first telephones is found here.

Throne Room
The king and queen would sit in state and receive their visitors here *(right)*. In 1895, however, in less happy times for the monarchy, Queen Lili'uokalani was put on trial in these august surroundings.

Dining Room
Formerly the Senate's meeting place, this much-restored room now contains custom-made sideboards, a commodious dining table, and an array of portraits depicting European heads of state.

Palace Galleries
This 50-room basement complex, with its chamberlain's offices, servants' quarters, and kitchens, was the heart of the palace. Today, royal treasures are presented here in state-of-the-art displays.

The Queen Composer

Lili'uokalani, arguably Hawai'i's best-loved queen *(see pp13 & 31)*, was also one of Hawai'i's most prolific composers. Born Lydia Kamake'eha Paki and known to her friends as Lili'u, she was already an accomplished musician and singer by the age of 15. While her best-known piece is surely the haunting *Aloha 'Oe*, she composed over 100 songs, many of which she had published.

🔟 Chinatown

The first Chinese immigrants arrived in Hawai'i in 1789, followed in 1852 by large numbers who came to work on O'ahu's plantations. On completion of their contracts, many gravitated to downtown Honolulu and opened restaurants, herb shops, and clubhouses. Fires in 1886 and 1900 nearly destroyed the neighborhood, and the area fell into decay. Today, after an extensive rejuvenation project, Chinatown is once again a thriving community where historic shrines and temples stand alongside colorful lei stands, herbal-medicine shops, vibrant farmers' markets, and trendy art galleries and restaurants.

A selection of dim sum

⭐ **For Chinatown tours**
see p42.

• *Chinatown Cultural Plaza: 100 N. Beretania St.; Map H2; 521 4934*
• *Honolulu Arts District: 1041 Nu'uanu Ave., Suite A; Map H3; 398 7990; www.artsdistrict honolulu.com; First Friday Gallery Walk: 5–9pm first Fri each month*
• *Hawaii Theatre Center: 1130 Bethel St.; Map H2; 528 0506; www. hawaiitheatre.com*
• *Izumo Taishakyo Mission: 215 N. Kukui St.; Map H1; 538 7778; 8am–5pm daily*
• *Foster Botanical Gardens: 50 N. Vineyard Blvd.; Map H1/J1; 522 7066; www1.honolulu. gov/parks/hbg/fbg.htm; 9am–4pm daily; adm: adults $5, children (6–12) $1, children under 6 free*
• *Contemporary Museum at First Hawaiian Bank: 999 Bishop St.; Map H2; 526 0232; 8:30am–4pm Mon–Thu, 8:30am–6pm Fri; free*

Top 10 Features

1. Dining
2. Open-air markets
3. Chinatown Cultural Plaza
4. Merchant Street Historic District
5. Honolulu Arts District
6. Festivals
7. Hawaii Theatre Center
8. Izumo Taishakyo Mission
9. Foster Botanical Gardens
10. Contemporary Museum at First Hawaiian Bank

1 Dining

Both visitors and Honolulu residents alike flock to Chinatown to sample the range of fresh Asian cuisine on offer. Vietnamese, Laotian, Chinese, Japanese, Thai, Filipino, Hawaiian, and Korean restaurants line the streets, offering a near endless supply of delicious and inexpensive culinary treats.

2 Open-air markets

A harmonious blend of Asian and Hawaiian culture, these lively and colorful markets sell fresh *leis*, traditional clothing, souvenirs, and art. In the morning, fresh produce stands overflow with fish, meat, candied fruits, dim sum, noodles, tea, duck eggs, char siu, and other delicacies.

Lion-dance performance to celebrate Chinese New Year

3 Chinatown Cultural Plaza

With an assortment of restaurants and vendors, the Cultural Plaza *(below)* is a microcosm of Chinatown. Kung fu and lion-dance performances are held here around Chinese New Year.

4 Merchant Street Historic District

Directly south of Chinatown, the city's earliest commercial center documents the city's commercial development between the 1850s and 1930s, covering a host of architectural styles. It was added to the National Register of Historic Places in 1973.

5 Honolulu Arts District

On the eastern edge of Chinatown, this is home to cultural institutions, performing-arts venues, galleries, and events such as the First Friday Gallery Walk.

6 Festivals

Chinatown celebrates Chinese New Year in traditional style and the fourth of July and New Year's Eve with fireworks. There are also 'ukulele contests and Cinco de Mayo parties.

7 Hawaii Theatre Center

The "Pride of the Pacific" *(below)* opened in 1922 and has hosted an impressive array of films and live performances, from local talent to big names. Allow time to explore the atmospheric interior.

9 Foster Botanical Gardens

Nearly 100,000 visitors annually pass through these historic grounds, enjoying the diverse botanical offerings. Guided tours are perfect for those curious about the exotic flowers and trees.

8 Izumo Taishakyo Mission

One of the few Shinto shrines in America (and the oldest in Hawai'i), this impressive wooden structure *(left)* was inspired by Japan's Shimane Prefecture's classical

Taisha Machi shrine. The Hiroshima Peace Bell is on view, and on New Year's Day the shrine is the site of local Shintoists' annual *hatsumōde* (celebration).

10 Contemporary Museum at First Hawaiian Bank

This collection of art, housed in the headquarters of Hawaii's oldest bank, features exhibitions by Hawaiian artists.

Rejuvenation

Chinatown was once Honolulu's seediest neighborhood, but the Historic District designation led to its rejuvenation and brought a cultural renaissance to the area. The neighborhood has sprung to life, with trendy lounges and tantalizing ethnic eateries rising up where once there were downtrodden bars and tacky tourist shops.

🔟 Honolulu Academy of Arts

Hawai'i's only general art museum, comprising 30 galleries, was founded in 1927 by the eclectic collector Anna Rice Cooke, whose home had become crammed with more than 4,500 pieces of artwork. The gracious stucco-and-tile building in the style islanders call "Territorial" was erected on the site of her original house.

Museum façade

⏺ **Doris Duke Theatre** at the academy is one of only two venues for independent and foreign films on O'ahu. Cozy, acoustically superior, and comfortable, this space also hosts concerts, lectures, and performances. For programming information, call 532 8768.

- Map M2
- 900 S. Beretania St.
- 532 8700
- www.honolulu academy.org
- 10am–4:30pm Tue–Sat, 1–5pm Sun
- Closed Mon
- Adm $10 (discounts for seniors, military, children – under 3s free); free first Wed and third Sun of every month
- Shangri La Center for Islamic Arts, 532 3685 (reservations); tours each Wed–Sat (they book months in advance); closed Sep; adm $25

Top 10 Highlights

1. Western Collection
2. East Meets West
3. Asian Paintings
4. Southeast Asian & Indian Collections
5. Art of the Pacific, Americas, & Africa
6. The Art of Hawai'i
7. Textiles Collection
8. Henry R. Luce Gallery
9. Arts of the Islamic World
10. Shangri La Center for Islamic Arts

Oceania collection

2 East Meets West

This group of objects is the product of a concept to which the Academy is deeply committed: the meeting of cultures. It is particularly apt since Hawai'i is one of those meeting places. Exhibits include trade goods and furnishings made in the East for Western use.

3 Asian Paintings

A centerpiece of the academy's Asian holdings is the James Michener Collection of *ukiyo-e* paintings *(such as the example below)*, which also includes some of Hokusai's *Thirty-six Views of Mt. Fuji*. The Asian Collection is equally strong in Japanese scrolls and Ming-dynasty Chinese paintings.

1 Western Collection

Based initially on Cooke's gifts, this collection has grown to over 15,000 pieces. It is particularly strong in American works in all media and French 19th- and 20th-century painting, such as the Polynesian themes painted by Gauguin *(above)*.

4 Southeast Asian & Indian Collections

A gallery of Indian art, mostly collected by a wealthy Indian family who live in Honolulu, has everything from a magnificent carved door to wedding attire. Southeast Asian items range from shrouds to headdresses, and sculptures to ceramics. Indonesian pieces appear in both the Asian and Islamic collections.

5 Art of the Pacific, Americas, & Africa

Masks, effigies, figurines, statuary, everyday tools, religious artifacts, and other pieces from the Americas, Oceania, and Africa are displayed in separate galleries and in periodic special exhibits.

6 The Art of Hawai'i

This group, made up primarily of paintings, graphic arts, decorative arts, and sculpture, includes many of the most recognized images in the islands, such as Theodore Wores' *The Lei Maker* (1902, *below*).

7 Textiles Collection

The Academy's textile collection is immense, with only a small selection on display at any time. While the focus is on Asia, there are also fine examples of Pacific *tapa* cloth. Japanese *kabuki* costumes, an emperor's *jifu* (robe), saris, and everyday clothing are well represented.

9 Arts of the Islamic World

In conjunction with the Doris Duke Foundation for Islamic Art, this gallery is made up primarily of pieces from Duke's broad-reaching collection – furnishings, woven objects, decorative pottery, and printed papers. Tours of Shangri La begin here.

Chinese robe in the textiles collection

8 Henry R. Luce Gallery

This area of the Academy incorporates a large space for changing exhibits, the Hawaiian art collection, workshops, and the Academy's offices.

Orientation

The Academy is arranged around a series of sun-splashed courtyards. Facing the central courtyard as you enter, the European and East-Meets-West collections are to the right; Asian artwork is on the left. The Henry R. Luce Pavilion, Art of the Americas, and the comprehensive Islamic and Indian galleries are at the rear.

10 Shangri La Center for Islamic Arts

Tours of Doris Duke's 1930s-era seaside mansion at Black Point begin at the Academy with a film, followed by a van ride to her home (*right*).

🔟 Kalākaua Avenue

Waikīkī's two-mile-long oceanfront street, running from Ala Wai bridge to the magnificent Diamond Head, epitomizes the dream of Hawai'i – gentle surf and vibrant nightlife. Named for Hawai'i's playful last king, the street is lined with storied hotels, parks, and a host of attractions. The city has spruced up the street at Waikīkī Beach with plantings, seating areas, and a waterfall that's a favorite "photo op" spot.

Waikīkī trolley bus

Top 10 Sights

1. Royal Hawaiian Hotel
2. Sheraton Moana Surfrider Hotel
3. Waikīkī Beach
4. Duke Kahanamoku
5. Kapi'olani Park
6. Honolulu Zoo
7. Royal Hawaiian Centerl
8. Waikīkī Aquarium
9. War Memorial Natatorium
10. Diamond Head

Waikīkī Avenue

🍀 Take a picnic to Kapi'olani Park, where you can sprawl out on the grassy areas.

• Map G5–M7
• Royal Hawaiian Hotel: 2259 Kalākaua Ave., 923 7311
• Sheraton Moana Surfrider Hotel: 2365 Kalākaua Ave., 922 3111
• Zoo: 151 Kapahulu Ave., 971 7171, 9am–4:30pm daily; www.honoluluzoo.org
• Aquarium: 2777 Kalākaua Ave., 923 9741, 9am–4:30pm daily; http://waquarium.org

1 Royal Hawaiian Hotel

The "Pink Lady" *(right)* retains her cache. Even if you're not staying at this most famous of Waikīkī hotels *(see p116)*, you can take afternoon tea on the veranda or visit the famed Mai Tai Bar.

2 Sheraton Moana Surfrider Hotel

The porticoed "White Lady" *(see p116)* dates back to 1901. The Sunday champagne brunch on the veranda is legendary; an evening at the Beach Bar an absolute must.

Royal Hawaiian Hotel

3 Waikīkī Beach

It's all happening here just as it has for more than a century – beachboys giving surf lessons; old-timers playing checkers; canoe teams practicing; locals mingling with tourists in the gentle waves. The whole beach is open *(left)*, including the areas in front of the Royal and Moana hotels *(see also pp46 & 72)*.

Duke Kahanamoku

At Kūhiō Beach, the figure hung with *lei (left)* is Duke Pa'oa Kahanamoku, a pioneer surfer and Hawai'i's "Ambassador of Aloha" in the 1960s.

Kapi'olani Park

This 170-acre parcel was dedicated by King Kalākaua in 1877. It was a military encampment in World War II, but today is a place for families, music, and festivals *(right)*.

Honolulu Zoo

A compact zoo with a number of warm habitats *(below; see also p40)*. Check out the Komodo dragon. If time permits, take a backstage zookeeper tour, moonlight walk, or overnight campout.

Royal Hawaiian Center

This upscale shopping center, with more than 100 shops and eateries, stands out for its cultural-enrichment programs, such as *lei* making and hula lessons.

Waikīkī Aquarium

Popular with youngsters for its sharks and Hawaiian monk seals, the aquarium *(right)* is involved in conservation projects, and hosts reef walks and excursions.

War Memorial Natatorium

This 1920s Beaux Arts saltwater pool was intended as a living memorial to World War I servicemen. It fell into disrepair, however, and though it has been partially restored, its future is uncertain.

Diamond Head

The crater at the end of Kalākaua Avenue is two-thirds of a mile across; its brow is 761 feet high, and its summit circumference is two miles. Take the 1.5-mile trail to its top for sweeping views *(see also pp42 & 73)*.

How to "Go Diamond Head"

The extinct Diamond Head volcano crater is so important an icon that Oahuans tell direction by it – "Go diamond head" means "Go East" to locals. Want to sound Hawaiian? Call it "Kaimana Hila" (KYE-mah-na HEE-la), an English borrowing that literally translates as "Diamond Hill." It's also the name of a popular hula.

TOP 10 South Shore

O'ahu's South Shore changes rapidly from suburb to barely touched landscapes of azure bays, botanical gardens, and a shoreline from which whales can be seen in the winter surf. Though close to the city's action, the coast has almost no services – no stores and few restrooms. An occasional lunchwagon at Sandy Beach and a snack stand at Hanauma Bay provide respite.

Hanauma Bay

Sandy Beach

🌀 **For a day on the sunny South Shore, pack a cooler of ice, water, drinks, and snacks; bring sunscreen, hats, and sturdy shoes; rent or buy snorkeling gear for Hanauma Bay.**

• Map F5–6
• Hanauma Bay Marine Center: 396 4229, 6am–7pm Wed–Mon; adm $7.50 ($1 to park); go early or after 2pm
• Koko Head Trail: the access road is just to the right of the Hanauma Bay entrance
• Koko Crater Trail: park at the lot for the Hālona Blow Hole, then walk back along Kalaniana'ole Hwy until you see the trail angle off through the Job Corps Training Center property
• Koko Crater Botanical Garden: Access is off Kealahou St., off Kalaniana'ole Hwy; sunrise to sunset daily; free; for guided hikes call 522 7063

Top 10 Sights

1. Hanauma Bay Marine Center
2. Hanauma Bay Beach
3. Hanauma Bay Underwater Park
4. Toilet Bowl
5. Koko Head Trail
6. Koko Crater Trail
7. Koko Crater Botanical Garden
8. Hālona Blow Hole
9. Sandy Beach
10. Wawāmalu & Kaloko

1 Hanauma Bay Marine Center

Drifting aquatic plantlife, delicate coral, vibrant fish, green sea turtles, and rays can be seen in Hanauma Bay. A visit to this center is worthwhile and compelling to better understand the area's dangers and ecological fragility.

South Shore coastline

2 Hanauma Bay Beach

Though it remains a beautiful, palm-shaded beach *(left)*, Hanauma's popularity makes a visit worthwhile only if you also plan to experience the underwater park.

3 Hanauma Bay Underwater Park

Waders, novice snorkelers, and more experienced divers can all enjoy this extraordinary preserve equally. The central area of the park is the safest; strong currents exist three quarters of the way to either side, ready to surprise non-attentive snorkelers.

For more on Hanauma Bay's Marine Center see p38

Toilet Bowl
A rocky pool, known for its exciting churning action as waves wash in and out. Folks love to bob up and down in the maelstrom, but be warned: there have been injuries.

Koko Head Trail
This trail involves a ramble along a steep, paved road, followed by a scramble along the spine of Koko Head, then a downhill path for views of the shoreline and the sea (see p38).

Koko Crater Trail
Buffeted by wind and strewn with crumbly rocks, this exposed trail to the 1,200-ft crater is one you should approach with caution, good shoes, and a hat.

Koko Crater Botanical Garden
The magnificent scent of plumeria flowers (also known as frangipani, above) is the lasting impression to take away from this dry-land garden right inside Koko Crater.

Sandy Beach
Locals love this beach (above), and on weekends it's busy with body and boogie boarders. Just be aware that waves slam into the sloping sand beach with great force, resulting in many a broken bone.

Wawāmalu & Kaloko
These two beaches are fine for shoreline pleasures, such as sunbathing or flying a kite, but don't even think of taking on the killing shore break and swift currents.

Hālona Blow Hole
This lava tube sucks up water from below, then sends it shooting up (above; see also p39). You can climb down close to the blow hole, but it is very dangerous to go near the opening.

Koko Head

The peninsula by Hanauma Bay is formed out of two volcanic landmarks: Koko Crater and the peak at Koko Head. Koko was the traditional name of a canoe landing at the Wai'alae side of Koko Head. The crater is also called Kohelepelepe. Today, the area is part of a regional park.

For more on the South Shore see pp96–101

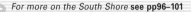

23

⭐ Kāne'ohe District

The area loosely known as Kāne'ohe is both commuting distance from Honolulu and a world away, the gateway to the North Shore and its country-style life. Many Native Hawaiians live here and the area is peppered with historic sites. You notice the difference at once – more pickup trucks, parked vehicles selling fresh fish and Hawaiian foods, and a slower pace.

Horseback riding, Kahalu'u

Kahalu'u Regional Park Beach

🌀 The three most direct routes to Kāne'ohe from town offer beautiful views. On the Pali Highway (H61), stop at the lookout. Likelike Highway (H63) is the quickest route, with spectacular scenery as you emerge from the tunnel. From H3, the entire Kāne'ohe area is laid out before you.

- Map E4
- Ho'omaluhia Botanical Garden: 45-680 Luluku Rd., Kāne'ohe; 233 7323, 9am–4pm daily; guided walks 10am Sat & 1pm Sun
- Ha'ikū Gardens: 46-336 Ha'ikū Rd., Kāne'ohe; 247 6605; www.haikugardens.com
- Valley of the Temples: 47-200 Kahekili Hwy, Kāne'ohe; 8am–4pm daily; adm $2 ($1 for seniors and children)
- He'eia State Park: 46-465 Kamehameha Highway, Kāne'ohe, 247 3156

Top 10 Sights

1. Ho'omaluhia Botanical Garden
2. Ha'ikū Gardens
3. Valley of the Temples Memorial Park
4. Byodo-in Temple
5. Mōkapu Peninsula
6. Moku O Lo'e (Coconut Island)
7. He'eia State Park
8. Kahalu'u Fishpond
9. Kahalu'u
10. Mokoli'i (Chinaman's Hat)

Ho'omaluhia Botanical Garden

The 400 fragrant acres of this park *(below)* also function as a flood-control facility. The area takes in themed plantings, trails, camp sites, a visitor center, and a lake.

Byodo-in Temple

Ha'ikū Gardens

Planted by an Englishman, this park has a small lake, groves of ginger and bamboo, a well-kept lawn, a gazebo, and a pavilion. It is a popular venue for wedding ceremonies.

Valley of the Temples Memorial Park

Yes, it's a cemetery but it's also a place to take in the islands' cultural diversity and the beauty of the Ko'olau mountains. It's not uncommon to see entire families picnicking near the graves of loved ones; graves of Buddhists are equipped with food and incense to honor the spirits.

Byodo-in Temple

At the rear of the memorial park, against the mountains, this other-worldly structure is worth the park admission alone. It's a scale replica of the 900-year-old temple at Uji in Japan, watched over by an immense incense-wreathed Buddha. Enjoy feeding the swans and banging the deep-toned gong.

5 Mōkapu Peninsula
Visible throughout the district, this peninsula is, alas, out of bounds because it's home to a military base. Despite the hum of aircraft, it's a beautiful sight *(above)*.

6 Moku O Lo'e (Coconut Island)
This islet has a varied history and is now the site of a biological research facility, famous for its study of marine life, especially coral.

8 Kahalu'u Fishpond
The 80-acre Kahalu'u Fishpond *(right)* is one of a handful of working ponds that date from a time when traditional Hawaiians farmed fish using rock walls fitted with *mākaha* – slatted gates that let fingerlings out but denied escape to larger fish.

9 Kahalu'u
Bordering Waihe'e Stream and straddling Kamehameha Highway, Kahalu'u Regional Park is something of a focus in the Kahalu'u area. Its many activities include ballfields, a gym and swimming pool, a beach park, boat launch, and canoe house.

10 Mokoli'i (Chinaman's Hat)
A lopsided conical island *(below)*, visible from He'eia to Kualoa, Mokoli'i is often visited by kayakers. It is said to be the remains of a giant *mo'o* (lizard god).

7 He'eia State Park
Perched on a hillside, this interpretive park hosts educational activities aimed at explaining the area's use as both an aquaculture center and a sacred site where spirits entered the afterlife.

Marine Corps Base Hawai'i

Kāne'ohe Bay is home to more than 10,000 U.S. Navy and Marine Corps personnel. The base's mid-Pacific location makes it ideal for deployment to the Far East. Historically, this same place – Moku-kapu to ancient Hawaiians – was called "sacred district" because Kamehameha I met his chiefs here.

Polynesian Cultural Center

Covering 42 acres on O'ahu's scenic north shore, the Polynesian Cultural Center provides an un-paralleled opportunity to experience seven Pacific Island nations in one place on a single day. Though undeniably kitsch in places, the center has been immensely popular since the 1970s and welcomes around one million guests annually.

Tongan dancers/musicians

🏝 It's recommended that visitors arrive before 1:30pm for an optimum experience of the entire center.

- Map D1
- 55-370 Kamehameha Highway, Lā'ie
- 293 3333 reservation system
- www.polynesia.com
- 12:30–9pm Mon–Sat; Cultural Villages close at 6:30pm
- General adm: adult $49.95, child $35.95; show package (includes dinner): adult $69.95, child $54.95. Dining & transportation packages also available

Top 10 Highlights

1. Tongan Village
2. Tahitian Village
3. Marquesan Exhibit
4. Hawaiian Village
5. Fijian Village
6. Maori Village
7. Samoan Village
8. Rainbows of Paradise
9. IMAX Theater
10. Hā: Breath of Life and the Ali'i Lū'au

Tahitian Village
A French territory since 1842, Tahiti is known for, among other things, its incredibly fast, hip-shaking dance, the *tamure*. You can learn the dance at the village, but if your hips aren't up to it, you can opt for the coconut bread-making instead.

Marquesan Exhibit
Made famous by artist Paul Gauguin, who spent his last years in the Marquesas, the culture of these islands is represented at the center through weaving and carving, tattoos, and Marquesan songs and dance.

Tongan Village
The only remaining kingdom in the Pacific, Tonga has been ruled by the Tupou family since 950. The center's Tongan Village features drumming, tapa cloth making, and a nose flute demonstration. And you can throw a spear on the village green!

House of the Gods, Fijian Village

Hawaiian Village
There is nothing more representative of Hawaiian culture than hula. And this is the place to try the dance for yourself and learn about the symbolism of the moves. You can also play Hawaiian versions of checkers and bowling at the village *(left)*.

5 Fijian Village

Fiji represents a cross-cultural mix of Polynesia and Melanesia. The center's Fijian Village features a tribal meeting house and an outrigger canoe, while the House of the Gods is the landmark for the whole center.

Entrance

6 Maori Village

Wall carvings conveying ancient stories about these great navigators are on display here, and you can also learn about the fierce-looking Maori facial tattoos and see the famous *haka* war dance.

7 Samoan Village

Robert Louis Stevenson, known in Samoa as Tusitala (story-teller), loved the people so much that he settled on Western Samoa to live out his days. You can find out how to climb coconut trees and open their husks at the Samoan village *(left)*.

9 IMAX Theater

The theater shows one film daily. Titles include *Coral Reef Adventure*, which highlights the importance of the ocean to the locals, and *Polynesian Odyssey*, which tells the story of the ancient Polynesians.

8 Rainbows of Paradise

Each day at 2:30pm, the quiet lagoons come alive. Dozens of Polynesians in traditional costume present an interpretation of 5,000 years of Pacific Island cultural lore in a rousing pageant *(above)*.

10 Hā: Breath of Life and the Aliʻi Lūʻau

The former is an exuberant Polynesian song and dance revue, featuring more than 100 performers; the latter a feast of traditional foods and contemporary entertainment.

The Mormon Connection

The center was established in 1963 by the Mormon Church of Jesus Christ of Latter-day Saints – there is a relatively high Mormon demographic in Hawaiʻi. The center's mission is twofold: to help preserve the cultural heritage of Polynesia and to provide jobs and scholarships for students at Brigham Young University. The school's Hawaiʻi campus is located next door.

Left **Plantation era** Right **Statehood tourist poster**

TOP10 Moments in History

1 Formation of the Islands

Each of the islands in the Hawaiian archipelago is actually the top of an underwater volcano. The oldest of the seven major islands (formed some 70 million years ago) is Kaua'i; the youngest Hawai'i, where the active Kīlauea volcano adds more landmass daily. A new island, Lō'ihi, is forming far below the ocean's surface, southeast of Hawai'i.

2 Polynesian Migration

Scholars believe that Marquesan voyagers first came to Hawai'i as early as the 4th century, with Tahitians arriving later, in the 13th. It was these two great waves of migration by skilled Polynesian seafarers that first populated the Hawaiian islands.

3 Western Contact

The landing of British explorer Captain James Cook at Kealakekua Bay on the island of Hawai'i in 1778 is generally acknowledged to be the first time Hawaiians had contact with westerners. There is evidence that Spanish ships sailed into island waters in the 16th century, but there are no records of any contact being made with the islanders.

4 King Kamehameha I Unites the Islands

An accomplished warrior chief from the island of Hawai'i, Kamehameha I waged war to conquer O'ahu and Maui, then forced the island of Kaua'i to cede to his dominion. Thus the islands were unified into the Kingdom of Hawai'i in 1809.

5 Missionaries Arrive

April 19, 1820 is a moment-ous (some would say notorious) date, when the first American missionaries arrived in Hawai'i. The first group was made up of 23 New England Congrega-tionalists, and they landed at Kailua on Hawai'i. Over the next 20 years, many more Christian mission-aries would follow, taking up residence on all the major islands.

6 The Plantation Era

Beginning in the mid-1800s, the American businessmen who first set up sugar cane production on the Hawaiian islands started importing contract laborers to work the plantations. Chinese workers were followed by Portuguese, Japanese, Latin American, Korean, and Filipino immigrants. The immigration of those groups led to the diverse ethnic mix found in the islands today.

Precontact statue

Previous pages **Ceremonial boat, Polynesian Cultural Center**

7 The Overthrow of the Hawaiian Monarchy

On January 17, 1893, Hawai'i's last queen, Lili'uokalani, was removed from her throne and placed under house arrest in 'Iolani Palace. The coup was the work of American businessmen based in Hawai'i, though it was not supported by U.S. President Grover Cleveland, a Democrat. He was unable to persuade the provisional government, led by Republican Sanford P. Dole, to restore the monarchy.

8 Pearl Harbor Attacked

It was a quiet, overcast Sunday morning when Japanese warplanes attacked the U.S. fleet anchored at Pearl Harbor. This shocking and stunning attack on December 7, 1941 marked the official entry of the United States into World War II *(see also pp8–9)*.

9 Tourism

They came first by ship and then by airplane, and by the late 1950s tourists were coming in increasing numbers, seeking the warmth and exotic beauty of Hawai'i, a place within easy reach of the West Coast of the U.S. mainland. Today, the islands host more than seven million visitors each year, arriving from every corner of the globe.

10 Statehood

Following several failed attempts, Hawai'i became the 50th state in the Union on August 21, 1959. William F. Quinn and James K. Kealoha were sworn in as the first elected governor and lieutenant governor of the new state. The occasion is marked each year by a state holiday, Admission Day, celebrated on the third Friday in August.

Influential Leaders

1 King Kamehameha I
The *ali'i* (chief) who in 1809 united the islands into the Kingdom of Hawai'i, after defeating Maui's *ali'i*, Kahekili.

2 King David Kalākaua
Affectionately known as the Merrie Monarch, David Kalākaua became king in 1874 and is credited with the revival of hula.

3 Bernice Pauahi Bishop
Granddaughter of Kamehameha I, whose name lives on in the Bishop Museum.

4 James Campbell
An early sugar baron who died in 1900; his estate is valued at over $2 billion dollars.

5 Loren Thurston
Transplanted mainland U.S. businessman and leader of the "Bayonet Revolution" of 1887, which ended the monarchy.

6 Queen Lili'uokalani
Hawai'i's last and one of its most beloved monarchs *(see also pp13 & 15)*. Her government was overthrown in 1893.

7 John Burns
A strong statehood advocate, John Burns was elected in 1962 to his first of three terms as governor of the State of Hawai'i.

8 Daniel Inouye
Hawai'i's first Congressman was elected to the Senate in 1962 and has since served seven consecutive terms.

9 John Waihe'e
The first governor of Hawaiian ancestry, he led the state from 1986 to 1990.

10 Nainoa Thompson
The navigator for the Polynesian Voyaging Society since the 1970s, he has revived traditional voyaging arts.

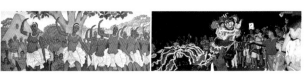

Left **Hula dancers from the 1940s** Right **Chinese Lion Dance**

🔟 Music & Dance Styles

Hula Kahiko

In this famous art form, hula dancers are accompanied by percussive instruments made from natural materials and the intonations of one or more chanters. Ancient hula began, it is believed, as a male preserve and as religious ritual.

Slack-key guitar playing

Traditional Hawaiian Chant

As an oral tradition, Hawaiian stories and family histories were related through chant *(oli)*. Ranging greatly in style, *oli* are used for scores of reasons, from prayers and lamentations to requests for permission to gather flora.

Hula 'Auana

When the practice of hula was revived during the reign of the Merrie Monarch, King David Kalākaua, a new dance style took center stage. Known as *hula 'auana* (modern hula), it is accompanied by instruments like the 'ukulele, guitar, standing bass, and singing voices.

It is more flowing in style than *hula kahiko*, and dancers generally wear western clothes.

Slack-Key Guitar

The term slack-key refers to a style of playing the guitar in which the strings are loosened, producing a jangly sound. Gabby Pahinui was, perhaps, the most famous of Hawai'i's slack-key masters – others included Raymond Kane and Sonny Chillingworth.

Steel Guitar

The Hawaiian steel guitar was born in the islands around the turn of the 20th century, but exactly where, when, and how is still a point of discussion. The instrument is held horizontally on the player's lap, and a sliding steel bar is used instead of fingers on the fret board. The sound was particularly big during the Sweet Leilani era.

The Sweet Leilani Era

From 1900 to the early 1940s was the era when U.S. mainland composers were greatly influenced by Hawai'i, mostly as a result of the way the islands were portrayed by Hollywood. This era – when songs like *Sweet Leilani, Yacka Hula Hickey Dula,* and *My Honolulu Lady*

Hula dancers

were composed – is called the *Hapa-Haole* or Sweet Leilani era.

Contemporary Hawaiian Music

The modern renaissance of the Hawaiian culture, which began in the late 1960s, continues to this day, with music playing a major role. The Brothers Cazimero, Ho'okena, the late Israel Kamakawiwo'ole, and Maui's own Keali'i Reichel have combined their astounding voices with modern instruments and classic Hawaiian poetic techniques to create a magnificent new sound.

O-Bon

O-Bon is a traditional Japanese religious observance but has evolved, as have so many cultural practices in the islands, into a more secular event. O-Bon dances honor deceased ancestors and are joyous occasions marked by drums, music, dances, and, nowadays, festival foods and fun activities.

Lion Dance

During February's Chinese New Year celebrations, the Lion Dance is performed all over Hawai'i. Acrobatic dancers don a lion costume and perform a dance to a steady – and very loud – drum beat designed to ward off evil and spread good fortune. Spectators fill red and gold envelopes with dollar bills and feed them to the lion to ensure future prosperity.

World Beat

As a miscellany of musical styles from around the world has made its way to the islands, so it is increasingly influencing musicians. Jawaiian describes a blend of reggae and Hawaiian music, and island rappers are now putting their own slant on hip-hop music.

Hawaiian Music and Dance Essentials

Pahu
Perhaps the most sacred of hula implements, *pahu* are drums, traditionally made using coconut tree trunk with a covering of sharkskin.

Ipu
A hollowed-out gourd that, in skilled hands, is used to keep the beat in hula.

'Ili'ili
Smooth stones – two are held in each hand and played by hula dancers in a style similar to Spanish castanets.

Pū'ili
Bamboo sticks, one end of each cut into a fringe so that they produce a rattling sound when played by hula dancers.

Kāla'au
Pairs of sticks of varying length that are struck against each other during dancing.

'Uli'uli
Gourd shakers that are filled with seeds and usually topped with feathers.

'Ukulele
A gift from the Portuguese that's now integral to modern Hawaiian music. "Jumping flea" was how Hawaiians first described the sound.

Guitar
Whether slack-key, steel, acoustic, or electric, the guitar is essential to Hawaiian music.

Standing Bass
As in jazz ensembles, the standing bass has found its way into a lot of contemporary Hawaiian music.

Falsetto Voice
Most easily described as male vocalists singing above their regular range, there is arguably no sweeter sound than the Hawaiian falsetto.

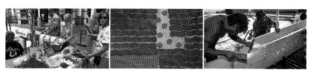

Left **Crafts stall** Center **Quilt pattern** Right **Canoe building**

Craft Traditions

Weaving

Traditionally, women are the weavers in Hawai'i, and many of the old everyday objects they created from *lau hala* (leaves of the pandanus tree) and the minutely thin *makaloa* (sedge grass) are considered works of art today. *Lau hala* mats, hats, and handbags are easily found in craft shops, but *makaloa* is now something of a rarity.

Coconut frond hat

Lei Making

There's no more enduring symbol of Hawai'i than the *lei* (garland). In the past, permanent *lei* were made from shells, seeds, bone, and feathers, and temporary *lei* from vines and leaves. Today, colorful and fragrant flowers like plumeria and tuberose are most associated with this craft.

Featherwork

Cloaks, *lei*, headware, and *kāhili* (standards) for the *ali'i* (chief) were all once fashioned from feathers. The birds were trapped so that specific feathers could be plucked, and then the creatures were released. Yellow, red, and black were the colors most often used. Today, artisans still craft *lei* of feathers from pheasant and other introduced species.

***Lei* making**

Kapa

Used throughout old Polynesia for clothing, blankets, and decoration, Hawaiian *kapa* is made from the bark of the *wauke*, or paper mulberry tree. The process, which is restricted to women, involves pounding the bark repeatedly into paper-thin sheets that are then decorated using bamboo tools and plant dyes.

Stonework

Stones are an important part of Hawaiian cultural life, used in practical situations (such as building) and for spiritual needs (such as the fertility and birthing stones found on all the islands). Because stones are so highly regarded, visitors are asked not to remove them from their setting.

Fishing Nets

Olonā fiber, derived from a native shrub, was commonly used in the old days to make fishing nets (a practice performed by men only). Strong and durable though it was, man-made materials such as nylon replaced *olonā* in the 20th century.

Canoe Building

As in all Hawaiian cultural practices, there is much ritual surrounding the building of a canoe, another of the

'Ukulele fabrication

men's arts. Traditionally, canoes are made of *koa* and always from one log, carefully selected by the boat builder. The craft is still very much alive today.

8 'Ukulele Making

A Portuguese import of the late 19th century, the 'ukulele quickly found its place in Hawaiian music. 'Ukulele making is still a respected art in Hawai'i, and companies like Kamaka on O'ahu and Mele 'Ukulele on Maui produce high-quality, hand-crafted instruments.

9 Hula Implements

The implements used by hula dancers and their accompanying chanters have changed little over hundreds of years. Though some enthusiasts still craft their own implements, hula supply shops on all the islands now allow dancers with busy 21st-century lives to purchase many of the items needed (though the materials used may not always be traditional these days).

10 Quilting

Among the many traditions brought by the missionaries was quilting. Not surprisingly, Hawaiian women took to the art form and made it their own, replacing New England designs with gorgeous renderings of local flora and fauna.

Top 10 Lei Styles

1 Haku
Flowers, leaves, or fruit are braided onto three strands of *ti* or other natural fiber. *Haku lei* are most often worn around the head or on a hat.

2 Hili
Hili are braided *lei* made from a single plant material such as *ti* leaf or *maile*.

3 Humupapa
Flowers are sewn onto plant material such as dried banana leaves *(lau hala)*.

4 Kui
Today's most familiar *lei* – flowers strung together with needle and thread.

5 Kīpu'u
Short lengths of vines or long-stemmed leaves are knotted together.

6 Wili
Plant materials are attached to a natural backing by winding fiber around them. *Wili lei* have no knots until the very end.

7 Lei Hulu (Feather Lei)
Traditionally made of feathers from now mostly extinct or endangered native birds, the art continues using feathers from common birds.

8 Lei Pūpū (Shell Lei)
These range from *puka-shell lei*, wildly popular in the 1970s, to museum-quality *Ni'ihau-shell lei*, worth many thousands of dollars.

9 Seed Lei
Simple, single-stranded Job's Tears and intricately crafted *wiliwili-seed lei* are popular examples of this type.

10 Contemporary Lei
From silk and ribbon to yarn, currency, and even candy, contemporary *lei* are made for every occasion.

Left **Chinese New Year** Right **King Kamehameha Day Celebration**

☷⓾ Festivals

1 Chinese New Year
The sound of hundreds of thousands of firecrackers, the time-honored Lion Dance, and bountiful feasts mark Chinese New Year in the islands. It takes place in early February, and anyone can take part.

Lei Day

Park. Other activities include concerts, a Folklife Festival and an international hula competition.

2 Cherry Blossom Festival
This long-running springtime festival perpetuates the rich heritage of Japanese culture through activities like the Heritage Fair and the Hawai'i International Taiko (Drum) Festival. The celebration culminates with the Festival Ball where a Cherry Blossom Queen and her Court are chosen.

3 Lei Day
"May Day is Lei Day" say the lyrics of a popular Hawaiian song. Not that anyone in the islands needs an excuse to make, wear, or give a *lei*, but May 1st is the day when master *lei* makers showcase their amazing skills.

4 King Kamehameha Day Celebration
The highlight of the June events marking the King's birthday is O'ahu's colorful Floral Parade, which wends its way through Honolulu and Waikīkī, ending at Kapi'olani

5 Lantern Floating Ceremony
People flock to Ala Moana Beach Park each Memorial Day (last Monday in May) for the setting adrift of thousands of flickering lanterns in remembrance of those who gave their lives in conflict. Guests are encouraged to pray for a peaceful, harmonious future.

6 Prince Lot Hula Festival
Held annually on the third Saturday in July at lovely Moanalua Gardens, the festival is the largest and oldest non-competitive hula event in Hawai'i. It is named for Prince Lot, who reigned briefly as King Kamehameha V and was known for his commitment to the perpetuation of the Hawaiian culture.

Prince Lot Hula Festival

7 Hawai'i State Farm Fair

Sponsored by the Hawai'i Farm Bureau Federation, this county-style fair is held in mid-July to the delight of locals and visitors alike. Perennial favorites are the Country Market, which sells fresh produce from Island farms, the 4-H Livestock Exhibition, and the Plant Sale.

8 Aloha Festivals

Contemporary Hawai'i is celebrated from mid-September to mid-October every year. The festivities begin on O'ahu and move through the island chain with at least a week-long celebration at every stop. A "royal court" is chosen on each island, and there are floral parades, concerts, and craft fairs.

9 Hawai'i International Film Festival

The fact that renowned Chicago-based film critic Roger Ebert attends regularly is enough to give HIFF some well-deserved national weight. Started in 1981 as a project of the East-West Center when seven films from six countries were screened, today HIFF screens approximately 100 international films at two-dozen locations on six islands.

10 Honolulu City Lights

Children of all ages look forward anxiously to the evening in early December when the switch is flipped that lights up the city Christmas tree, signals the start of the Honolulu City Lights Electric Light Parade, illuminates the entire civic center area, and, of course, marks the beginning of the holiday season. The light displays, which adorn all city department buildings, are truly magical.

Top 10 Sports Events

1 Sony Open
Prestigious PGA Tournament played in January.

2 NFL Pro Bowl
A football game between the NFC and AFC all-stars caps off a week of festivities in late January/early February.

3 Great Aloha Run
Tens of thousands run the 8-mile race on President's Day (February), many for charity.

4 Transpacific Yacht Race
Better known simply as the Transpac, dozens of yachts race from the California coast to Hawai'i every other July.

5 Nā Wahine O Ke Kai/Moloka'i Hoe
First the women in late September, then the men in mid-October paddle outriggers across the Island channels.

6 UH Sports
Locals go hog-wild over the amateur volleyball, football, and other games at the University of Hawai'i.

7 Honolulu Marathon
Each December some 25,000 international runners enjoy O'ahu's scenic course.

8 Hawai'i Bowl
Two top-ranked college football teams get in on the action around Christmas in sunny Honolulu.

9 Outrigger Rainbow Classic Basketball Tournament
A favorite holiday tournament features the beloved University basketball team competing against Mainland counterparts.

10 Vans Triple Crown of Surfing
Professional surfers from all over the world gather on the North Shore in Dec/Jan.

Left **Punchbowl** Right **Koko Head Botanical Park**

Natural Features

Punchbowl

The 150,000-year-old cone above the city of Honolulu has three identities. Its Hawaiian name, Pūowaina, means "hill of sacrifice" – it was an ancient place of ritual and royal burial. Punchbowl, its English name, refers to its shape. Today it is also the final resting place for more than 35,000 veterans of American wars in Asia and the Pacific. ◉ Map L1 • Cemetery 8am–6:30pm daily • American Legion tours (fee); 532 3720

Hālona blow hole

Diamond Head

Arguably the most recognizable landmark in all of Hawai'i, this gracefully aging volcanic remnant was named by the Hawaiians Le'ahi, "brow of the yellowfin tuna," for its shape. Its English name refers to the glinting calcite minerals, which were mistaken for diamonds. The interior has housed military operations and hosted rock concerts. A trail offers sweeping views. ◉ Map C7 • 6am–6pm daily (last entrance 4:30pm) • Adm • Walking tour 9am Sat (free); 948 3299

Koko Head

Not the most impressive peak on O'ahu, but its homely bulk is a landmark. Nearby, Koko Crater rises to 1,200 ft. A panoramic two-mile hike is reached through a botanical park – the trail is wind-swept, narrow, and crumbly. ◉ Map F6

Hanauma Bay

This keyhole-shaped Nature Preserve is so beautiful and popular that the state has had to restrict access to protect it. You enter through a $13 million Marine Education Center and

Diamond Head

Hanauma Bay

view a video before descending to the bay via tram for snorkeling and sunning. ◈ *Map F6 • 396 4229 • 6am–7pm Wed–Mon • Adm • Access denied when lot is full; go early or after 2pm*

Hālona Blow Hole
A lava tube that funnels geysers of sea water high into the air, this dramatic feature is one to observe with care, preferably from the scenic pullout above it. Many who have hazarded too near have been injured or killed. From November through March, watch for spouting whales out to sea, as well as spouting water. ◈ *Map F5*

Ko'olau Mountain Range
The wind- and water-cut Ko'olaus are the subject of countless Hawaiian chants and songs. This Windward-side mountain range (the name means "windward"), so green and dramatic, forms O'ahu's spine from southeast to northwest. ◈ *Map C2–F4*

Wai'anae Mountain Range
Composed of the remnants of the Wai'anae volcano, said to have grown quiescent 2.5 million years ago, this range is the higher of the two on O'ahu, reaching above 4,000 ft. The mountains here have a distinct wet (east) and dry side (west). ◈ *Map B3–4*

Mount Ka'ala
This, the tallest peak on O'ahu at 4,020 ft, is a preserve where indigenous birds and boggy plants prosper in the mist. On its slopes and at its feet, sandalwood once prospered, before the forests were decimated by Hawaiian royalty greedy for Chinese silks and other trade goods. ◈ *Map B3*

Sacred Falls, Kaliuwa'a
Unfortunately, one of the most beautiful and beloved landmarks on O'ahu, located in Punalu'u, is off-limits for the foreseeable future. A tragic landslide in 1999 that killed eight people forced closure of the park. The state has found no practical way to assure safety in this narrow, cliff-lined defile. ◈ *Map D2*

Banzai Pipeline
Just off the beach once known as Paumalū, the Banzai Pipeline is the name given to a spectacular winter surf break, the result of a shallow coral reef that serves as a sudden stopping point for deep water currents sweeping inland. The name Banzai comes from the battle cry of Japanese warriors, and was first applied to the waves here during the narration of the late 1950s film *Surf Safari*. (See p77.) ◈ *Map C1*

Left **Wahiawā Botanical Gardens** Center **Lili'uokalani Botanical Gardens** Right **Honolulu Zoo**

🔟 Gardens & Nature Parks

1 Foster Botanical Gardens

Planted by a pioneering botanist in the 1850s, nurtured by an amateur gardener, and willed to the city in 1931, this easily accessed city garden includes plantings of orchids and palms, and rare and endangered tropical plants. ⓢ *50 N. Vineyard Blvd., Honolulu • Map H1 • 9am–4pm daily • 522 7066 • Adm*

Foster Botanical Gardens

2 Lili'uokalani Botanical Gardens

Bequeathed to her people by the last monarch of Hawai'i, the garden focuses on native plants. The site includes portions of Nu'uanu Valley. ⓢ *North Kuakini St., Honolulu • Map E5 • 7am–5pm daily • 522 7060 • Free*

3 Hawai'i Nature Center

This non-profit conservation group encourages children to look after the environment. Weekend family programs including interpretive hikes, earth care projects and nature adventures are held at the center in a picturesque ravine in Makiki Valley. ⓢ *2131 Makiki Heights Dr., Honolulu • Map C6 • 955 0100*

4 Lyon Arboretum

Named for Harold L. Lyon, longtime director of botanical gardens in Honolulu, this University facility is both a field station and a public garden of tropical plants, native plants, conservation biology, and Hawaiian ethnobotany. Classes, workshops and outings are offered. ⓢ *3860 Mānoa Rd, Honolulu • Map C6 • 8am–4pm Mon–Fri, 9am–3pm Sat • 988 0456 • www.lyonarboretum.com*

5 Honolulu Zoo

The venerable zoological garden in Waikīkī incorporates savanna and tropical forest areas, birds and reptiles of the Pacific islands, and a children's zoo. A summer concert series is hosted on the grounds. ⓢ *151 Kapahulu Ave., Honolulu • Map M7 • 9am–4:30pm daily • www.honoluluzoo.org • 971 7171 • Adm*

6 Moanalua Gardens

This non-profit environmental education center in historic

Lili'uokalani Botanical Gardens

Ka'ena Point Natural Area Reserve

pressures of multiple uses such as off-road vehicles, fishermen, hikers, shell-collectors, and traditional Hawaiian practitioners, Ka'ena Point park is a narrow strip of land that connects the two ends of Farrington Highway (at Mokule'ia and Yokohama Bay). Hike a muddy, rutted road, catching sight of small bays and beaches until you reach O'ahu's end, a tumbled landscape of sand dunes, rocks, and waves. ✎ Map A2

Kamananui Valley offers walks and operates an award-winning school program. The free Prince Lot Hula Festival *(see p36)* takes place each July on a traditional grassy hula *pā* (mound) in the shady park. ✎ 1352 Pineapple Place, Honolulu • Map E6 • 839 5334

Kawainui Marsh
Rescued from proposed development in the 1960s, this 830-acre wetland offers abundant wildlife and archaeological sites. Access is available from a flood control dike but the city is contemplating an ambitious perimeter. ✎ Map E4

Wahiawā Botanical Gardens
Opened to the public in 1957, the rain forest garden nestles in a ravine on a high plateau. The focus is on tropical plants that prosper in a cooler environment. ✎ 1396 California Ave., Wahiawā • Map C3 • 9am–4pm daily • 621 5463 • Free • Guided tours available

Ka'ena Point Natural Area Reserve
Largely unimproved and subject to the

Mt. Ka'ala Natural Area Reserve
This preserve is alongside a military reservation and readily reached by road. However, the paved route is off-limits to civilians, who must climb challenging trails to reach the misty bog in a bowl-like hollow atop O'ahu's highest peak. The area has become a safe haven for native plants and wildlife; a boardwalk allows viewing without causing damage to the fragile ecosystems. It's best to consult detailed hiking guides before setting out. ✎ Map B3

Left **Mt. Tantalus forest, Makiki Valley** Center **Trail sign** Right **Hikers on the Diamond Head Trail**

Treks

1 Honolulu Walking Tours

The American Institute of Architects (AIA) leads two-hour Saturday tours (starting at 9am) of downtown Honolulu, taking in examples of various architectural styles. Chinatown tours are led by the Hawai'i Heritage Center on Wednesdays and Fridays (9:30–11:30am). Ohana Tours also offers walking tours of Chinatown and downtown Honolulu on weekday mornings.
◈ AIA: 545 4242 • Hawai'i Heritage Center: 521 2749 • Ohana Tours: 866 204 7331

A shrine in Chinatown

2 Judd Memorial Trail

This easy one-hour trek in Nu'uanu Valley is a tribute to the forester Charles S. Judd, who planted the pines here in the 1930s. The pond is less picturesquely named Jackass Ginger after a donkey that used to be tethered in a nearby ginger grove. ◈ Reached from Nu'uanu Pali Drive near Ilanawai Condominium • Map E5

3 Makiki Valley Loop Trail

This two-mile loop, incorporating short segments of three longer routes – Kane'aole Trail, Makiki Valley Trail, and Maunalaha Trail – has been cleared, planted with native vegetation, and equipped with directional signs.
◈ Enter via Hawai'i Nature Center, off Makiki Heights Drive • Map C6

4 Diamond Head Trail

Extremely steep in places, dusty and dark in others, this two-mile hike ends in a series of viewing platforms. The landscape spread before you, from Koko Head in the east to the curve of the Leeward Coast on the west, is worth the energy expended (see also p73). ◈ The trail begins at the Diamond Head State Monument parking lot, off Diamond Head Road at 18th Street in Kaimuki • Map C7

5 Makapu'u Lighthouse Trail

Makapu'u Point is the spot where prevailing currents from the deep ocean are split by the land, resulting in interesting wave

Diamond Head Trail

Riding at Kualoa Ranch

action. An easy but breezy one-mile walk along an abandoned road takes you to a World War II pillbox and Makapu'u Lighthouse. Watch for whales in winter. ☙ *Park at the Makapu'u Wayside • Map F5*

Maunawili Demonstration Trail

Requiring half a day and someone to pick you up at the end, the Maunawili Trail extends from Pali Highway above Kailua to a back road in Waimānalo. It is a moderately easy 10-mile hike for which you will be rewarded with a rain forest valley, then views of the island's windward side. ☙ *Map F4*

Ha'iku Stairway

The 2,210-ft ascent to a Ko'olau peak here is via a metal staircase built by the military for a now-defunct communications facility. After falling into disrepair, the trail closed due to a dispute over parking in the neighborhood. However, despite this, many still find a way to "unofficially" climb it, so access at your own discretion. Not to be attempted by the weak of heart, the stairway offers views normally available only to ardent hikers. ☙ *Map E4*

Kualoa Ranch Horse Trails

The Kualoa Ranch & Activity Club offers daily one- and two-hour rides on this historic, 150-year-old family ranch *(see p92)*. One-hour rides traverse the base of the Ko'olau Mountains; two-hour rides delve into wide Ka'a'awa Valley. These are suitable for inexperienced riders. ☙ *49-560 Kamehameha Hwy, Kāne'ohe • Map E3 • www.kualoa.com • 237 7321*

Ka'ena Point Trail

This five-mile, two-hour trek along the muddy remains of the shore highway offers pole-fishing sites, shelling in small inlets during low tide, and glimpses of birds, dolphins, and whales *(see also p79)*. ☙ *The trailhead is at the Mokulē'ia end of Farrington Hwy • Map A2*

'Aiea Loop Trail

A family-friendly hike in and out of the gullies in 'Aiea Valley will familiarize you with vegetation such as *'uluhe* fern and *'ōhi'a lehua*. (Don't pick the scarlet sprays of *lehua* flowers, custom says, or it will rain.) ☙ *From the top of 'Aiea Heights Drive, enter Keaïwa State Park and park at the top • Map D4*

Left Pōka'i Bay Beach Center Kayaking, Kailua Right Boogie boarding, Waikīkī

Beaches

Ala Moana

Ala Moana
The most popular beach park in urban Honolulu offers 76 acres of activities, though most folks simply swim, wade and sunbathe on the man-made sandy beach. If you do swim here, you must take care, as the channel is deep and, at low tide, you don't have to venture far to be caught in strong currents. Facilities onshore include food concessions, tennis courts, lifeguard towers, and softball fields. ◈ Map B6

Waikīkī
Possibly the most famous beach in the world, Waikīkī has had a facelift, with the installation of lush, grassy berms to block street noise, and an eye-catching waterfall feature. The beach remains prime people-watching territory, as well as being a gentle and safe place for swimming and learning to surf. ◈ Map L7

Sans Souci
Grown up around a small resort where Robert Louis Stevenson stayed in the 1880s, Sans Souci is good for swimming, bodysurfing, and boogie boarding. Safe, calm, and shallow, it's popular with families and also with the gay community. ◈ Map E6

Ka'alāwai Beach
Reached from a public right of way at the end of Kulamanu Place off Kāhala Avenue and Diamond Head Road, this narrow, white sand beach is protected by a reef and is safe for swimming and snorkeling. It's also used for diving, pole fishing and throw-netting, while surfers make spectacular use of breaks in the reef. ◈ Map E6

Wai'alae Beach County Park
More popular for picnics and weddings than for swimming, this Kāhala beach is hemmed in by coral but offers access to coveted windsurfing areas and fishing holes. Watch out for – and keep small children away from – the deep, sometimes fast-flowing channel cut by Wai'alae Stream as it enters the sea.
◈ Map E6

Waikīkī

Previous pages Surfers, North Shore

Hale'iwa Beach

most beaches, Oneawa (with roadside parking) and Kalama (which has a parking lot), are accessed through Kailua neighborhoods. Kailua Beach Park has parking lots, food concessions, a volleyball court, picnic tables, and lifeguard towers. You can surf, windsurf, swim, boat, kayak, canoe, snorkel, and dive here, and the view of Nā Mokulua ("the mokes," as locals call these tiny islets) is the icing on the cake. ⬡ Map F4

Hale'iwa Ali'i
A popular beach park for family picnics, swimming, and surfing offshore at Pua'ena Point. The site has restrooms, a shady pavilion, plenty of food concessions, lifeguards, and sports fields too. ⬡ Map B2

Pōka'i Bay Beach
This beautiful beach is the calmest and safest place for swimming in Wai'anae, so it's no surprise to find it frequently thronged. It also has an unfortunate but deserved reputation as a place where car break-ins and beach burglaries occur, so take extra care with your belongings. ⬡ Map A4

Bellows Field Beach
Open to the public on weekends and national holidays, this beach park within a military reservation is prized for its broad shelf of powder-fine white sand, turquoise waters and ironwood-shaded campgrounds. Perfect for novice surfers, but watch out for stinging Portuguese man o'war jellyfish.
⬡ Map F5 • Camping by permit only

Lanikai Beach
Frequently voted one of the world's best beaches, Lanikai is reached through beach access trails in the ritzy Lanikai neighborhood along Mokulua Drive. It's flat and sandy, quite narrow in spots, and popular for swimming, boating, diving, and snorkeling. ⬡ Map F4

Kailua Beach
Two miles of golden sand fringe Kailua Bay, which is divided into three sections. The northern-

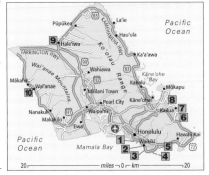

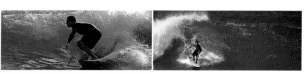

Left **Waikīkī surfer** Right **The surf at Ka'ena Point**

🔟 Surfing Beaches

Kaka'ako Waterfront Park/Point Panic

Unless you're highly skilled on a board and ready to join the elite who paddle out to Point Panic every day, this park is strictly for spectators. There's no beach, swimming is dangerous because the break crashes into the retaining wall, and sharks haunt the area. However, a broad pathway extends the length of the park offering great views, and picnic pavilions are clustered along it. This is also a favorite spot for watching celebratory firework displays over Waikīkī. ◈ Map B6

Ala Moana Beach

This area is popular for surfing because if offers a range of challenges from easy and slow Canoes to the more frisky Queen's, Paradise, and Populars areas. Locals who work in Waikīkī hit the waves before and after work. ◈ Map B6

Sandy Beach

"Sandy's" is the bodyboarding capital of O'ahu. Unfortunately, it is also the site of a lot of serious accidents and frequent rescues. A steep drop-off at the sand's edge means that waves are always pounding here, so only the most experienced should take on this surf, and everyone should take care of the treacherous back-wash, which frequently catches waders off-guard. ◈ Map F5

Makapu'u

The slow rolling shoulders of the waves and the lack of a reef below make this spot ideal for bodysurfing, plus board surfing is prohibited to prevent collisions. But watch out during high winter surf, and take heed of flag warnings from the lifeguards. ◈ Map F5

Sunset Beach

In winter, this wide, golden strand is piled high, forming a steep, natural amphitheater for watching surfers attack the awesome waves. In summer, changing tides flatten the beach out, making it more sunbathing-friendly. All year long, though, dangerous currents make swimming risky. There are park facilities across the street. ◈ Map C1

Makapu'u

'Ehukai

6 'Ehukai
'Ehukai ("sea spray" in Hawaiian) is safe for swimming during spring and summer, but during the fall and winter the board surfers take over and it becomes the unofficial viewing stand for observing the action at the world-famous Banzai Pipeline (see below) just to the left of the beach park. ◎ Map C1

7 Banzai Pipeline
A shallow coral reef extending out from the beach fronting Ke Nui Road throws up waves of tremendous power and steepness – so powerful that no one thought they could be ridden until the 1960s. Injuries from wiping out on the reef are numerous, but surfers can't resist these monsters. "Banzai", by the way, was the final cry of Japanese kamikaze pilots. ◎ Map C1

8 Waimea Bay
A beach with two personalities. Calm as a bathtub in summer, it's ideal for swimming, kayaking, and snorkeling. Come October and on until April, this beach (where Captain Cook first landed on O'ahu) is crowded with open-mouthed visitors watching surfers from around the world ride the wild surf. ◎ Map B1

9 Ka'ena Point State Park
Until the introduction of tow-in surfing, the mammoth waves of Ka'ena Point remained tantalizingly off limits to surfers because of the impossibility of paddling out from the rock-fringed, current-tossed shore. A north swell at Lae o Ka'ena results in 30–40-ft waves and brings out the most daring sorts. ◎ Map A2 • Reached via a 2.5 mile walk

10 Mākaha
Site of the Mākaha International Surfing Contest, the beach here is steep-sloped and wide, with lots of golden sand and deep waters close to shore. The well-formed waves range from medium in the off-season to VERY large in the winter. Stray boards can be a hazard to swimmers. ◎ Map A3

Mākaha

Left **Mākaha Golf Course** Right **Pali Golf Course**

Golf Courses

Ala Wai Golf Course

Ala Wai Golf Course

The world's busiest course is also one of the most loved in Hawai'i for its balance of challenge and playability – tradewinds may beat your ball back and slow play can test your patience, but the course is flat, there's little water, and many friendly locals. 404 Kapahulu, Waikīkī • 737 7387 • Map L5

Hawai'i Prince Golf Course

Affiliated with the Hawai'i Prince Hotel, and played frequently by visitors from Japan, this Arnold Palmer-designed course offers 27 subtly challenging holes. The flattish terrain is bedeviled by winds, tight fairways, and lots of water. 91-1200 Ft. Weaver Rd., 'Ewa Beach • 944 4567 • Map C5

'Ewa Beach Golf Club

This enjoyable semi-private course designed by Robin Nelson manages to retain the character of the historic dryland 'Ewa Plain with its *kiawe* trees and preserved archaeological sites. The tight, manicured fairways and ubiquitous bunkers offer a fair challenge-to-reward ratio. 91-050 Ft. Weaver Rd., 'Ewa Beach • 689 6565 • Map C5

Ko Olina Golf Course

This emerald oasis carved out of a dusty plain by designer Ted Robinson is considered one of O'ahu's most beautiful and challenging courses. It is also equipped with gorgeous distractions, including waterfalls and black swans. Expensive, but lots of discounts available. 92-1220 Ali'inui Dr., Kapolei • 676 5300 Ext. 1 • Map B5

Mākaha Resort Golf Club

This course in a historic valley over-looked by the island's highest point, Mt. Ka'ala, is worth the

Ko Olina Golf Course

Mākaha Golf Course

drive. Eight water hazards, 107 bunkers and a treacherous wind call for strategic thinking. An easier sister course is next door. ✎ 84-626 Mākaha Valley Road, Wai'anae • 695 9544 • Map A4

The Golf Courses at Turtle Bay

Two courses are showcased on this 880-acre resort on O'ahu's remote North Shore. The George Fazio Course has wide fairways and deep bunkers; the Palmer Course (by Arnie, of course) incorporates a "tropical links" of sun, wind, and sand on the front nine and a forested upland nine on the back. ✎ 57-091 Kamehameha Hwy, Kahuku • 293 8574 • Map D1

Ko'olau Golf Club

Golfers travel a long and winding road at this course, nestled among the foothills of the dramatic Ko'olau mountain range. It has been rated among the top 100 courses by Golf Magazine and named O'ahu's best by Golf Digest. Bring lots of extra golf balls and prepare for long

holes, water hazards, and a difficult layout. ✎ 45-550 Kiona'ole Rd., Kāne'ohe, 247 7088 • Map E4

Pali Golf Course

In the absence of water hazards and bunkers, the challenge of this undulating landscape is wet and often windy weather. But even duffers can enjoy meandering down swale and up hillside on sunny days. ✎ 45-050 Kamehameha Highway • 266 7612 • Map E4

Olomana Golf Links

Though it's called a links, this much-played windward side course is in view of, but not right by, the ocean. It's pretty, with the mountains as a backdrop and a network of ponds, but keep your eye on the ball and watch out for those little lakes. ✎ 41-1801 Kalaniana'ole Highway, Waimānalo, 259 7926 • Map F5

Hawai'i Kai Championship Golf Course

This coastal course is a windswept beauty, with narrow fairways, lots of sand, and an ocean view from every tee. Be sure to sign your name on the leaves of the milo or "message" tree. A shorter Executive Course is also available. ✎ 8902 Kalaniana'ole Highway, Maunalua, 395 2358 • Map F5

Island courses are always busy, so make reservations first. Seven days in advance is the maximum allowed by most municipal courses.

51

Left **Kayaking** Right **Street life, Chinatown**

🔟 Adventures

1 Gliding and Skydiving at Mokulē'ia
Air adventures at Dillingham Airfield include gliding, skydiving, and scenic flights *(see opposite)*. Choose from a 20-minute single-person glider flight to long scenic flights and lessons. ◎ *Dillingham Airfield past Waialua on Farrington Highway, Rte. 930, at Mokulē'ia*

2 Parasailing at Waikīkī
Hundreds of visitors a day experience the thrill of parasailing – sitting, strapped in a harness attached to a parachute, pulled by a boat, high above the waves.

3 Spa-Hopping (Ko Olina to Waikīkī)
Every variety and description of spa is available on O'ahu from European-style hydrotherapy to

Jet skiing

Balinese flower soaking tubs and beauty-oriented treatments. *(See pp54–5.)*

4 Jet Skiiing at Maunalua Bay
Jet-powered personal watercraft are a noisy – and some would say environmentally unsound – but enjoyable way to skim over the water with the feeling of flying. By law, jet skis are restricted to weekday, daytime hours. Ask about ski/parasailing combo packages.

5 Kayaking Kailua and Kāne'ohe
Locals favor kayaking along the Windward Coast, where small islets offer interesting scenery, and there's a popular sandbar in Kāne'ohe Bay. But many of the islets are bird sanctuaries where landing is prohibited.

6 Guided Hikes
Three non-profit groups, the Sierra Club (538 6616), the Nature Conservancy

The Windward Coast

(537 4508), and Hawaiian Trail and Mountain Club (674 1459), offer frequent hikes with the last group definitely on the hardier side.

Walking Tours

Regular walking tours of downtown, Chinatown, the Capitol District, Waikīkī, and the University campus are offered by various non-profit groups (see p42). A free map, the *Honolulu Historic Trail*, offers a self-guided tour.

Polo at Waimānalo and Mokulē'ia

Polo came to Hawai'i with the moneyed elite, and two polo grounds continue to operate on O'ahu. From June to October, matches are held at 2pm on Sundays. *Honolulu Polo Club, Waimānalo Polo Grounds (across from Bellows Beach) • Mokulē'ia Polo Club, 411 Farrington Highway in Mokulē'ia*

The Lū'au Experience

To experience an authentic Hawaiian feast *(lū'au)*, you have to find a family giving one. If that's not possible, try the Polynesian Cultural Center (see pp26–7) or other commercial operations. *Paradise Cove Lū'au, Ko Olina (842 5911) • Germaine's Lū'au, 91-119 Olai St., Kapolei (949 6626) • Royal Lū'au at the Royal Hawaiian Hotel, Waikīkī (931 7194), Mon only*

Shopping Mo'ili'ili/Kaimukī

Some of the most wonderful shops in the city are missed by many visitors. Head along South King Street in the 2700 block in Mo'ili'ili and on Wai'alae Avenue from 9th to 13th Streets in Kaimukī to discover everything from sophisticated hand-printed dresses to Hawaiian instruments and craft supplies.

Top 10 Rental Places and Commercial Tours

1 Soar Hawai'i Sailplanes
Operates at Dillingham Airfield.
637 3147 • www.soarhawaii.com

2 Original Glider
Rent a glider at Dillingham.
637 0207 • www.honolulusoaring.com

3 Skydive Hawai'i
Also at Dillingham Airfield, flights for experienced and novice skydivers. 637 9700 • www.skydivehawaii.com

4 Hawaiian Parasail
This recognized expert offers daily flights lasting eight to 10 minutes for around $40. Flights depart from Kewalo Basin with free pickup from Waikīkī Hotels. 591 1280

5 X-Treme Parasail
This company offers parasailing, fishing expeditions, jet ski rentals, and more. 737 3599 • www.xtremeparasail.com

6 Sea Breeze Parasailing
Operator based at Maunalua Bay. 396 0100 • www.seabreezewatersports.com

7 Hawai'i Watersports
Also at Maunalua Bay, offering a variety of rental equipment. 395 3773 • www.hawaiiwatersportscenter.com

8 Bob Twogood Kayaks Hawai'i
Reputable firm on the Windward Coast. 262 5656 • www.twogoodkayaks.com

9 Kailua Sailboards and Kayaks
Another good firm. 262 2555 • www.kailuasailboards.com

10 Hawaii Ecotourism Association
For commercial operations offering guided hikes, consult this association. 954 2910 • www.hawaiiecotourism.org

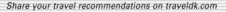

Left **24-Hour Fitness** Right **Ampy's**

🔟 Spas and Fitness Centers

1 24-Hour Fitness
As the name implies, this national chain offers a 'round the clock opportunity to work up a sweat. There are three clubs in Honolulu, one in Waikīkī, and four others dotted around O'ahu; most offer short-term passes. ✆ 923 9090
• www.24HourFitness.com

Paul Brown Salon and Day Spa

2 Paul Brown Salon and Day Spa
Two of Paul Brown's locations – one at Victoria Ward Center in Honolulu and the other at Waikele – are probably the most comprehensive and arguably the best of the independent day spas on O'ahu. ✆ 591 1881
• www.paulbrownhawaii.com

3 Serenity Spa Hawai'i
Located in the Outrigger Reef on the Beach Hotel *(see p116)*, you can charge your spa services to your room if you're a guest at any of the 23 Outrigger or 'Ohana properties. Massages

Ampy's

are offered poolside, while pampering wedding packages are a popular way to feel treated like *ali'i* (royalty). ✆ 2169 Kālia Rd., Diamond Head Tower • 926 2882
• serenityspahawaii.com

4 Ampy's A Day Spa
An award-winning day spa, Ampy's specializes in massage, body treatments, and facials, including the latest laser and dermabrasion techniques. Owner Ampy and her daughter Nicole both have European training. Enjoy a single treatment or a spa package. ✆ 1441 Kapi'olani Boulevard, Suite 377, 946 3838
• www.Ampys.com

5 Allure Hair Studio and Day Spa
One of Honolulu's leading spas, this one bills itself as an "experience center." A full range of pampering treatments is offered, with Aveda brand products to the fore.
✆ 2801 E. Mānoa Rd. • 988 3350
• www.allurehawaii.com

6 Clark Hatch Physical Fitness Center

With a network of centers throughout Asia and the Pacific, founder Clark Hatch's philosophy is "total fitness." Trained instructors create individual programs to promote a lifetime of well-being.
🕾 745 Fort St. • 536 7205
• www.clarkhatchfitness.com

7 Heaven on Earth Downtown Day Spa

The place of respite for harried downtown workers is equally agreeable to harried tourists in need of a stress-relieving massage. Owner Lora Nakai wants the feeling of wellness to last, and encourages therapists to impart helpful tips to clients.
🕾 Bishop Square, 1050 Alakea St. • 599 5501 • www.heavenonearthhawaii.com

8 Aloha Healing Arts

A skilled massage therapist with almost two decades of experience, Fran Rose offers Swedish massage, reflexology, shiatsu, sports massage, acupressure, and iridology. 🕾 1831 Ala Moana Blvd., No. 202 • 386 1820
• www.alohahealingarts.com

9 Marsha Nadalin Salon & Spa

If chic and upscale Kahala Mall is on your list of shopping stops, you can be rejuvenated at this day spa right in the shopping center. Men's services are available, too. 🕾 Kahala Mall • 737 8505

10 The Lomi Shop

When you've shopped until you're ready to drop at Windward Mall, duck into The Lomi Shop, which specializes in traditional Hawaiian massage techniques. Try a reviving 10-minute foot massage. 🕾 Windward Mall • 234 5664

Top 10 Health and Beauty Treatments

1 **Steam/Sauna** The steam room is wet, the sauna dry, and either one will open the body's pores in readiness for other treatments.

2 **Botanical Baths** Aromatherapy oils, herbs, and seaweeds are added to whirlpool tubs to either calm or re-energize the body.

3 **Herbal Scrubs** Scrubs use ingredients such as native red clay and island sea salts to exfoliate, detoxify, and soften the skin.

4 **Herbal Wraps** Wraps use herbs and the application of heat to draw out impurities from the skin.

5 **Massage** Shiatsu, Swedish, and Thai styles are available, but why not try Hawai'i's traditional lomilomi or the newer Pōhaku (stone) massage.

6 **Facials** Designed to clean and rehydrate the face; choices depend on skin type and individual needs.

7 **Aromatherapy** Integrated into many spa treatments, natural fragrances are used to invoke a specific mood or feeling.

8 **Manicure/Pedicure** The perfect way to end a day at the spa, manicures and pedicures always include a short hand and/or foot massage.

9 **Makeup** Every salon has experts on hand for a professional application of makeup.

10 **Fitness** All gyms and many spas have work-out machines, free weights, pools, and fitness classes.

Left *Poi* with fish Center **Shave ice** Right **Fruit stall**

🔟 Local Dishes

Sushi

1 Poi
The staple of the Hawaiian diet, *poi* is made by pounding to a paste the corm of the *taro* or *kalo* plant – a task that is strictly a male preserve. Traditional Hawaiians believe their culture to be descended from a *kalo* plant, signifying the symbolic importance of this food.

2 Kālua Pork
The centerpiece of any *lū'au*, or feast, is the whole pig, slow-roasted *(kālua)* in an underground oven – an *imu*. The meat literally falls from the bones. The same cooking method works equally well with turkey, squash, and sweet potatoes.

3 Plate Lunch
Meat, two scoops of rice, and macaroni salad. Those are the three essential elements of the plate lunch. Sold on every street corner in Hawai'i, it represents the melding of cultures, and the meat comes in many varieties, from teriyaki beef to pork and variously prepared chicken.

4 Sushi, Sashimi, and Poke
The primary Japanese culinary influences are sashimi (sliced raw fish) and sushi (raw fish, shellfish, or vegetables, served on top of, or rolled with, rice). *Poke*, the Hawaiian word for diced or chopped, is Hawai'i's version of Tahitian *poisson cru* and Latin American *ceviche*. These delicious raw fish-based dishes are available everywhere from fine dining restaurants to local supermarkets.

5 Noodles and Rice
Few meals in Hawai'i are served without rice, and those that are usually come with noodles. Indeed, noodles in hot broth with pork and green onions is a common dish for breakfast, lunch, or dinner, and leftover dinner rice often reappears as fried rice for the next day's breakfast.

6 Portuguese Sweet Bread and Bean Soup
Fresh from the oven and slathered with creamy butter is the best way to enjoy this wonderful bread, brought by Hawai'i's Portuguese immigrants. Originally baked in outdoor brick ovens, it is now available at markets throughout the islands. Every

Lū'au (feast)

family in Hawai'i, whether of Portuguese heritage or not, has its own Portuguese bean soup recipe. Brimming with beans, meat, and vegetables, it can be a hearty meal unto itself, especially when accompanied by a thick slice of sweet bread.

Kim Chee
Brought by Hawai'i's Korean immigrants, *kim chee* is simply pickled cabbage, but for those who love hot – that is, very hot – flavors, it is a "must try." Traditionally, the cabbage is stored in tightly sealed jars and buried in the ground, then dug up as and when needed.

Tropical Fruit
Mango, papaya, guava, *liliko'i* (passion fruit), bananas, and, of course, pineapple. Pure and simple right off the tree, blended into a delicious fruit smoothie, or transformed into an amazing dessert, these are truly paradisiacal flavors.

Shave Ice
It has other names in other places – snow cone is one – but it is simply small chips of ice, flavored with one or more of myriad syrups, served in a paper cone. Cool and refreshing on a hot summer day, the rainbow variety shave ice has become a virtual symbol of Hawai'i.

Spam
Yes, it's true. One of the most maligned foods in history is one of Hawai'i's most popular and beloved. Canned Spiced Ham (SPAM) was originally known as a military staple since it's easy to keep for long periods of time. It is, perhaps, the large military presence in Hawai'i that first accounted for its curious popularity in the islands.

Local Food Stops

1 Little Village Noodle House
An adorable place, the menu offering a full range of regional Chinese specialties. 1113 Smith St., Honolulu • Map H3

2 Gulick Delicatessen & Coffee Shop
The quintessential plate lunch place, with piled-high specials daily. 1512 Gulick Ave., Honolulu • Map D5

3 Side Street Inn
After work hangout of Honolulu's chefs, offering savory bar food. 1225 Hopaka, Honolulu • Map E6

4 Kaka'ako Kitchen
A plate lunch place owned by a high-end chef. Great pastries too. 1200 Ala Moana Blvd., Honolulu • Map B6

5 Rainbow Drive-In
This has been a go-to spot for plate lunches and Hawaiian staples for decades. 3308 Kanaina Ave., Honolulu • Map E6

6 Helena's Hawaiian Food
Helena's has made some of the best traditional Hawaiian food since 1946. 1240 N. School St., Honolulu • Map D5

7 Tokkuri-Tei
A Japanese izakaya (tavern) with an innovative East-West menu. 611 Kapahulu Ave., Honolulu • Map M7

8 Big City Diner
The deal here is burgers – BIG burgers. 3569 Wai'alae Ave., Honolulu • Map E6

9 Palace Saimin
The best place for Hawai'i's favorite comfort food: steaming bowls of noodles. 1256 N. King St., Honolulu • Map G1

10 Zippy's Restaurants
A widespread chain of two dozen O'ahu-style diners, serving simple, hearty food.

Left **La Mer** Right **Alan Wong's Restaurant**

🔟 Restaurants

1 Chai's Island Bistro

Exceptionally well prepared Asian fusion food, music by some of the islands' best-known entertainers, classy interior decor, and courtyard dining characterize this orchid-bedecked spot *(see p69).* ✪ *Aloha Tower Marketplace, Honolulu • Map H4 • 585 0011 • $$$$*

Chef Mavro

2 Sansei Seafood Restaurant & Sushi Bar

Sushi bar, fine dining restaurant, fashionable cocktail lounge, karaoke palace – Sansei is all these. The name means third generation and implies the East-West sophistication that the grandchildren of the immigrant generation have achieved. ✪ *Waikīkī Beach Marriott Resort & Spa – 2552 Kalākaua Ave., Honolulu • Map M7 • 931 6286 • $$$*

3 DK Steak House

The Waikīkī Marriott hosts a steakhouse experience that rivals any in the state, complete with in-house dry aged beef and a unique wine list. Take a balcony table for breathtaking views of Waikīkī Beach. ✪ *Waikīkī Beach Marriott Resort, 2552 Kalākaua Ave., Honolulu • Map M7 • 931 6280 • $$$$$*

4 Chef Mavro

This award-winning French-with-an-island-touch restaurant expresses the character of owner George Mavrothassitis – precise, passionate and absolutely individual. Exceptional wines by the glass are matched to each dish, and the service is impeccable *(see p69).* ✪ *1969 S. King St., Honolulu • Map M3 • 944 4714 • $$$$$*

5 Alan Wong's Restaurant

Hailed by many as Hawai'i's best restaurant, Alan Wong's marries local preferences with a formal setting. The food – unusual seafood preparations and amazing sauces – is delicious; the atmosphere relaxed and convivial. Great wine list *(see p69).* ✪ *1857 S. King St., Honolulu • Map M3 • 949 2526 • $$$$$*

6 Michel's

Old World elegance, sunset views of Waikīkī, and outstanding professional service make Michel's a favorite of romantics (many a proposal has taken place here). Authentic French fare and an inviting Sunday brunch satisfy gourmands. ✪ *2895 Kalākaua Ave., Honolulu • Map M7 • 923 6552 • $$$$$*

For more great restaurants and the key to price categories see pp69, 74, 81, 89, 95 & 101

7 La Mer

The best and most authentically French restaurant in Hawai'i makes lavish use of both local seafood and imported delicacies to create "cuisine de soleil," a cuisine of the sun with a distinctly Provençal bent. Formal dress. ◈ *Halekulani Hotel, 2199 Kālia Rd., Honolulu • Map J7 • 923 2311 • $$$$$*

8 3660 on the Rise

With an understanding for what Hawaiians like, this compact, ever-busy neighborhood bistro has specialties such as Hawaiian clay salt steak. They offer small plates, vegetarian options, and tasting menus, too. ◈ *3660 Wai'alae Ave., Honolulu • Map E6 • 737 1177 • Dinner only; closed Mon • $$$$*

9 Hoku's

An airy wood-paneled room, a view of the ocean, and a multicultural menu that ranges from tandoori specialties to wok cooking – "rustic international cuisine," as they describe it. ◈ *Kahala Hotel & Resort, 5000 Kāhala Ave., Honolulu • Map E6 • 739 8780 • $$$$$*

10 Roy's Restaurant

Roy Yamaguchi founded the first O'ahu restaurant of note in 1988. Here he offers the same spicy mixture that is his signature – creative cuisine that roams from Japan to Mexico. ◈ *6600 Kalaniana'ole Hwy., Honolulu • Map E6 • 396 7697 • $$$$*

Roy's Restaurant

Top 10 Regional Ingredients

1 Local Greens
Small farms grow dozens of varieties of lettuce and greens for Hawai'i's restaurants.

2 Vine-Ripened Tomatoes
Much juicier and tastier than their mainland cousins. Growers on all the islands now nurture this important ingredient.

3 Moi
Once enjoyed exclusively by *ali'i* (royalty), this small, delicate fish is now on menus throughout the islands.

4 Tropical Fruit
Chefs make excellent use of pineapple, papaya, guava, *liliko'i*, and lychee in salsas, sauces, and desserts.

5 Local Fish
Myriad varieties of local fish – like *mahimahi, ahi, opakapaka, onaga* – forms the foundation of Hawai'i cuisine.

6 Moloka'i Sweet Potatoes
With their brilliant purple flesh, these wonderful potatoes add color as well as flavor to dishes.

7 Corn
Chefs delight in using sweet, locally grown corn – both white and yellow corn is cultivated in the islands.

8 Slipper Lobster
Smaller than their Maine cousins; it is the sweet tail meat that is prized most.

9 Pohole
These bright green, crunchy, and delicious ferns grow in East Maui and are often served with tomatoes.

10 Local Meat
Beef, lamb, even elk and venison are produced by Hawai'i ranches and used extensively by local chefs.

AROUND
O'AHU

AROUND O'AHU

Left **Yacht harbor** Center **Chai's Island Bistro** Right **Hilton Hawaiian Village**

Honolulu

ONOLULU SOMETIMES GETS A BAD RAP *for being overcrowded, traffic-bound, parking-starved, and noisy. It is all of those things, but in an island kind of way, which is to say, it's not nearly as busy as almost any other major U.S. city. Honolulu's civic role is both that of state capital and seat of the City and County of Honolulu government, but, above all, this is a cosmopolitan center. Full of historic interest, the city is a great jumping-off point for all kinds of tourism, from guided walks to inter-island cruises. Though downtown tends to go dark after 5pm, its daytime life is all you could ask for, while the port and Chinatown districts stay lively into the small hours.*

View of Honolulu

🔟 Sights

1. Statue of Lili'uokalani
2. Aloha Tower Marketplace
3. O'ahu Cemetery
4. Royal Mausoleum
5. Nu'uanu Pali Lookout
6. Queen Emma Summer Palace
7. Punchbowl Cemetery
8. Contemporary Museum
9. Nu'uanu Cultural District
10. Kaka'ako Waterfront Park

See also pp10–19

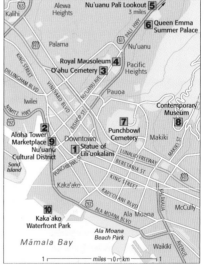

Previous pages **He'eia and Kane'ohe** *(see p91)*

1 Statue of Lili'uokalani

Weighted with *lei* (garlands) and symbolism, this exceptionally life-like bronze sculpture of Hawai'i's last queen stands on the south grounds of the State Capitol *(see pp12–13)*. In her hand she holds a copy of her evocative composition *Aloha 'Oe*, the 1893 Constitution, and the *Kumu Lipo*, Hawai'i's creation story. *Ho'okupu* (gift offerings) are often left

Statue of Lili'uokalani

here by sovereignty activists who revere this queen, who was forced to give up the monarchy under protest. ◈ *Map J3*

2 Aloha Tower Marketplace

This well-designed shopping complex in Honolulu Harbor has not been a success for its shops but is great for restaurants, nightlife, and free noontime entertainment. The 10-story tower, built in 1926 and standing at 184 ft, was once the tallest building in the islands. Today, visitors can take an elevator to the top floor for stunning views over the harbor and mountains. ◈ *Pier 9, Honolulu Harbor • Map H4 • 528 5700 • 9am–9pm daily (to 6pm Sun) • www.alohatower.com*

3 O'ahu Cemetery

The gravestones of this hillside resting place founded in 1844 read like a who's who of Hawai'i history, from the humble to the high-class. Nanette Napoleon, "the cemetery lady," has written a guidebook and leads periodic tours – both are worth seeking out. ◈ *2162 Nu'uanu Ave. • Map B6 • 538 1538 • 7am–6pm daily • Free • www.oahu cemetery.org*

4 Royal Mausoleum

The mausoleum is overseen by Hawai'i's only hereditary state office because the sacred duty to look after the graves is based on genealogy. It contains the bones of post-contact Hawaiian royalty, except for Kamehameha Nui, who was interred in an unknown Hawai'i Island location in accordance with custom, and Liholiho, whose grave is at Kawaiaha'o. A *koa*-lined coral block chapel dating to 1865 forms the cemetery's centerpiece, surrounded by the graves and vaults of the various family groups. ◈ *2261 Nu'uanu Ave. • Map B6 • 536 7602 • Mon–Fri • Free*

Left **Monument at Punchbowl Cemetery** Right **Royal Mausoleum**

Nu'uanu Pali Lookout

Famous as much for its hair-flying winds as for its blood-soaked history, this vantage point is where Kamehameha the Conqueror did final battle with O'ahu warriors *(see p30)*. The latter either jumped to their deaths or fought until they were pushed over the cliff edge rather than give in. This atmospheric site is sometimes cold and misty, but always spectacular and spooky. ⬡ *Off Pali Highway*

Queen Emma Summer Palace

Hānaiakamalama, a modest white, wood-frame house with high ceilings and deep porches, was the perfect warm-weather retreat, just far enough up the Nu'uanu Heights from Honolulu to catch chilly breezes. Queen Emma (née Rooke), who married King Kamehameha IV in 1856, inherited the home from her uncle. It was slated for destruction in the early 1900s, but saved by the Daughters of Hawai'i organization, who now operate it as a historical museum. ⬡ *2913 Pali Highway • Map C6 • 595 3167 • 9am–4pm daily • Adm*

Punchbowl Cemetery

Among O'ahu's most visited sites, the National Memorial Cemetery of the Pacific, spectacularly situated inside a

Bishop Street, part of Nu'uanu Cultural District

The Duck

That odd-looking, green-and-yellow vehicle that you are likely to see in downtown Honolulu is "The Duck," a WWII-vintage amphibious landing craft (DUKW was a manufacturer's acronym), refitted for open-air touring. Call 988 3825 to book a trip.

---

volcanic crater, offers extraordinary views and a humbling sense of the human sacrifice brought about by various Pacific wars. ⬡ *Map L1 • 2177 Puowaina Dr. • 532 3720 • 8am–6:30pm daily • American Legion members lead tours for a fee*

Contemporary Museum

A gracious family property on Makiki Heights overlooking Honolulu has become a world-class art center, showcasing cutting-edge work. There are delightful gardens, a quirky gift shop, and an exceptional café. ⬡ *2411 Makiki Heights Dr. • Map C6 • 526 1322 • 10am–4pm Tue–Sat, noon–4pm Sun • Adm (free third Thu of month)*

Queen Emma Summer Palace

For the Bishop Museum see pp10–11; 'Iolani Palace pp14–15; Honolulu Academy of Arts pp18–19

Punchbowl Cemetery

Nu'uanu Cultural District

Also known as Gallery Row, this area is a blended community of shops, restaurants, theaters, churches, and bars between downtown and Chinatown proper. The best time to get a sense of its rich life is on the first Friday evening of each month, when galleries and boutiques hold the First Friday Gallery Walk and stay open until 9pm, offering wine and *pūpū* (snacks), music, and opportunities to meet the artists. Even if your timing is off, you can pick up a Gallery Walk self-guided tour map at any area gallery. ◊ *Between Nimitz and Beretania, River and Bishop Sts. • Map H3*

Kaka'ako Waterfront Park

Honolulu's newest park – in its most-changed neighborhood on the waterfront between Sand Island and Ala Moana Beach Park – offers grassy knolls, views from 'Ewa to Diamond Head, picnic pavilions, a walking path, and a chance to watch the surfers up close at the infamous Point Panic. ◊ *Map B6*

Part of David Hockney's *L'Enfant et les Sortilèges* at the Contemporary Museum

Morning in Chinatown

Early Morning

🕐 Chinatown is best enjoyed right after breakfast, when the stands overflow with locally grown fruits and vegetables, imported Asian goods, Pacific fish, freshly made noodles, and every possible part of the chicken and pig. Wear comfortable shoes, dress for sunshine, and park at one of the less expensive municipal lots on Smith or Maunakea Streets.

The area between River and Nu'uanu, Beretania and King is great for small gifts — sandalwood soap, painted fans, kitchen tools, Chinese pottery, dried persimmons, and red-and-gold good luck banners. You can watch the butchers chop *char siu* (barbecue pork) so fast it looks like sleight of hand. Buy some fresh fruit to take back to the hotel.

Late Morning

When you've had enough, head *mauka* (toward the mountains) on River Street until you meet up with North Vineyard Street. There you'll find the gorgeously arrayed **Kuan Yin Temple** *(see p66)* and cool, green **Foster Botanical Gardens** *(see p40)*. Explore a bit before turning back toward Chinatown for lunch.

Try one of the popular restaurants in Chinatown, such as A Little Bit of Saigon (Vietnamese, on Nu'uanu), Mei Sum (dim sum on Smith), Little Village Noodle House (Chinese on Smith), To Chau (*pho* soup on River), or the stuffed French bread sandwiches at Ba-Le (on King).

For more on the Capitol District see pp12–13
For the Chinatown area see map H1–J2

Left **Alexander & Baldwin Building** Center **Academy Art Center** Right **Ala Wai Yacht Harbor**

🔟 Best of the Rest

Honolulu Harbor
Almost all of the state's waterborne traffic passes through here, and 98 percent of imports come to the islands by water. A great spot for watching harbor life is the patio of Gordon Biersch at the Aloha Tower Marketplace *(see p68)*. ◈ Map G3–H3

Alexander & Baldwin Building
The 1929 terracotta and tile A&B Building epitomizes Territorial period Hawaiian architecture. Asian, Mediterranean and island influences are filtered through the quintessential Hawaiian architects, C. W. Dickey and Hart Wood. ◈ Bishop and Merchant streets • Map J3

Ala Moana Center
With over 350 stores and regular live entertainment, this is Hawai'i's largest shopping mall and most visited destination. ◈ 1450 Ala Moana Blvd. • Map B6 • 955 9517

Kuan Yin Temple
Light bounces off the exterior of this Chinese place of worship; inside, incense drifts and the goddess of mercy looks on as devotees pray. ◈ 170 N. Vineyard Blvd. • Map H1 • 533 6361 • Daily • Free

Lili'uokalani Gardens
This garden was a retreat for the queen, where she picnicked to the tinkling sounds of Nu'uanu Stream. ◈ Waikahalulu Lane, off School St. in the Nu'uanu neighborhood • 522 7060 • Daily • Free

Academy Art Center
Exhibitions and sales of various art societies. The work is often very affordable. ◈ 1111 Victoria St. • 532 8741

TEMARI Center for Asian and Pacific Arts
This art group got its start when a few crafters met in 1979 to share their knowledge of Asian arts. Now the center hosts prestigious classes. ◈ 1754 Lusitana St. (Hongpa Hongwanji Temple) • Map K2 • 536 4566

University of Hawai'i
Two self-guided walking tours focus on the plant life and art work on the campus. ◈ Info from Campus Center: 956 7235 • www.hawaii.edu

Tantalus Drive
The loop drive from Makiki Street up Round Top Drive, and along Tantalus Drive is not to be missed – picnic along the way at Pu'u 'Ualaka'a Park. ◈ Map E5

Ala Wai Canal
With a wide path all along its length, the canal offers a lovely evening's walk, ending at the Ala Wai Yacht Harbor. ◈ Map G6

For more information about art exhibitions and classes in Honolulu, visit **www.temaricenter.com**

Left **Neal S. Blaisdell Concert Hall** Center **Hawaii Theatre** Right **Diamond Head Theatre**

🔟 Theaters & Music Venues

 Army Community Theatre
Though it's located on a military base, this venerable organization is a true community theater, attracting actors and audiences from around the island. Their standard fare is the familiar musical. ⌖ *Richardson Theatre, Ft. Shafter • 438 4480*

Hawaii Theatre Center
This one-time movie theater has been wonderfully renovated, and now offers a full and varied season of everything from *hula hālau* fundraisers to visiting dance companies. ⌖ *1130 Bethel St. • Map H2 • Box office: 528 0506*

Kumu Kahua
The focus of this 100-seat experimental theater is new work from around the Pacific.
⌖ *46 Merchant St. • Map H3 • 536 4441*

Tenney Theatre
A small theater that hosts frequent choral recitals. ⌖ *229 Queen Emma Sq. • Map J2 • 838 9885*

 Neal S. Blaisdell Arena
When Honolulu lands a rock show or traveling circus, this basic hall is where it happens. ⌖ *777 Ward Avo. • Map L3 • 591 2211*

Neal S. Blaisdell Concert Hall
The 2,185-seat concert hall is home of the Honolulu Symphony, the Hawai'i Opera Theatre, Ballet Hawai'i's annual holiday *Nutcracker*,

and most other symphonic events.
⌖ *777 Ward Ave. • Map L3 • 591 2211*

Mamiya Theatre
Mamiya, named after the pioneering heart surgeon who endowed it, is used for recitals, dance, and performances.
⌖ *3142 Wai'alae Ave. • 739 4886*

John F. Kennedy Theatre
The campus theater includes a 600-seat main theater and a smaller Earle Ernst Lab Theatre. The season includes plays and musicals, and Kabuki and Noh Japanese theater. ⌖ *1770 East-West Rd., UH campus • 956 7655*

Manoa Valley Theatre
This small but highly respected theater is a former church hall out in a graveyard in misty Mānoa Valley. ⌖ *2833 E. Mānoa Rd. • 988 6131*

Diamond Head Theatre
The largest of the community theaters offers beloved musicals to pidgin English fairy tales, contemporary drama to comedy.
⌖ *520 Makapu'u Ave., Kaimukī • 733 0274*

Around O'ahu – Honolulu

Left **Gordon Biersch Brewery** Right **Rumours Nightclub**

🔟 Bars and Clubs

Manifest
Modern coffee shop by day, trendy lounge by night, this Chinatown hangout is a favorite see-and-be-seen spot among the city's sophisticates. ◈ *32 N. Hotel St. • Map H2 • 523 7575*

Opium Den
With expertly crafted cocktails (pomegranate and lychee martinis are popular) and a DJ spinning dance tracks, this hip hangout in the Indigo restaurant *(see opposite)* is a hit with trendy locals.

Gordon Biersch
The pier-side bar becomes a club on weekends – one of the few where you can boogie out-doors. There's live music some-times, with the fare tending to contemporary rock. ◈ *Aloha Tower Marketplace • Map H4 • 599 4877*

Loft Gallery and Lounge
Huge paper lanterns, sheer curtains, and chandeliers make this one of the most attractive clubs on the island. The tiny nooks and couches are ideal for romantics. ◈ *115 Hotel St. • Map J3 • 688 8813*

Oceans 808
This dance club has weekly events and serves good food early evening. ◈ *500 Ala Moana, Restaurant Row • Map B6 • 587 5838*

The Dragon Upstairs
Some of the city's top jazz musicians congregate at this inti-mate Chinatown hideaway to jam through the night, much to the delight of local music lovers. ◈ *1038 Nu'uanu Ave. • Map H2 • 526 1411*

Ryan's Grill
Munch your way through the delicious *pūpū* (snacks) menu and be mesmerized by the colored bottles in the backbar. ◈ *Ward Center, 1200 Ala Moana • Map B6 • 591 9132*

Mai Tai Bar
Very much a local favorite, this bar has live Jawaiian (local reggae) music, comfy couches, and a lounge style. ◈ *Ala Moana Shopping Center • Map B6 • 947 2900*

Rumours Nightclub
This dress-up club, popular with locals and Japanese tourists, is packed with young things in tight outfits dancing to Top 40 pop and local rock. ◈ *Ala Moana Hotel, 410 Atkinson Dr. • Map G5 • 955 4811*

Anna Bannana's
Aging hippies and blues hounds adore this time-warped tavern, with its darts games, grizzled regulars, and upstairs weekend gigs. ◈ *2440 S. Beretania • Map L2 • 946 5190*

Recommend your favorite bar on traveldk.com

Price Categories

Price categories include a	**$** under $20
three-course meal for one,	**$$** $20–$30
a glass of house wine,	**$$$** $30–$45
and all unavoidable extra	**$$$$** $45–$60
charges including tax.	**$$$$$** over $60

Left **Asian cuisine at Chai's Island Bistro** Right **Chef Mavro**

Around O'ahu – Honolulu

🔟 Places to Eat

1 Sam Choy's Breakfast, Lunch, and Crab
Sam Choy creates updated versions of islanders' favorites, notably seafood. The huge portions and laid-back style are dearly loved by a loyal local clientele. ✆ 580 N. Nimitz Highway • Map G2 • 545 7979 • $$$

2 Indigo
Chef Glenn Chu has created a high-tone, pan-Asian restaurant, split between a cool, restrained dining room and a more casual patio. ✆ 1121 Nu'uanu, Chinatown • Map H2 • 521 2900 • Closed Sun & Mon • $$$$

3 Chai's Island Bistro
This beautiful, high-ceilinged, flower-bedecked restaurant, complete with fountain courtyard, serves well-presented Asian fusion cuisine (see p58). ✆ Aloha Tower Marketplace • Map H4 • 585 0011 • $$$$

4 Hiroshi Eurasion Tapas
Award-winning chef Hiroshi Fukui presents a fusion of European and Asian cuisines. The walls feature frequently changing works by local artists. ✆ 500 Ala Moana Blvd., Honolulu • Map B6 • 533 4476 • Dinner only • $$$

5 Kincaid's Fish, Chop and Steak House
Eat steak, fish, or lobster here overlooking Kewalo Basin. ✆ 1050 Ala Moana Blvd. • Map B6 • 591 2005 • $$$$

6 Kua'aina Sandwich Shop
This is famous for its burgers, piled with a range of toppings, from bacon and cheese to salsa and pineapple. ✆ Ward Village Shops, 1116 Auahi St. • Map M4 • 591 9133 • $

7 Café Sistina
Even if the Northern Italian food here wasn't scrumptious, you'd still have to go just to see chef-owner Sergio Mitrotti's wall and ceiling murals. ✆ 1314 S. King St. • Map M3 • 596 0061 • $$$

8 Chef Mavro
Small, award-winning restaurant offering "France-Hawai'i cuisine." Much focuses on the freshest local seafood (see p58.) ✆ 1969 S. King St. • Map M3 • 944 4714 • Dinner only • Closed Mon • $$$$$

9 Alan Wong's Restaurant
Probably the best restaurant in Hawai'i, where European style is married with the best island techniques (see p58.) ✆ 1857 S. King St. • Map M3 • 949 2526 • $$$$$

10 Leonard's Bakery
Founded in 1952, this beloved local bakery churns out warm, handmade malassadas (Portuguese doughnuts). ✆ 933 Kapahulu Ave. • Map M5 • 737 5591 • $

Note: Unless otherwise stated, all restaurants accept credit cards and serve vegetarian meals

69

Left **Beach life** Center **The waterfront at dusk** Right **U.S. Army Museum**

Waikīkī

WAIKĪKĪ, the famous resort area containing the most sought-after real estate in an island chain full of sought-after real estate, has undergone a facelift. Hundreds of millions of dollars have been plowed into renovations. Numerous hotels are upgrading; the International Market Place is returning to its romantic origins; the grassy walks along Waikīkī Beach now bloom with plantings; statuary has been erected commemorating historic figures; and the Kapi'olani Park Bandstand has been rebuilt. All the more reason the inhabitants say, "E komo mai!", or "Welcome!", to visitors.

Sights

1 Hawai'i Convention Center
2 U.S. Army Museum
3 Urasenke Teahouse
4 International Market Place
5 Waikīkī Beach
6 Kahuna (Wizard) Stones
7 Kūhiō Beach
8 King's Village
9 Kapi'olani Bandstand
10 Diamond Head Crater

Left **Outrigger Restaurant** Right **Hawai'i Convention Center**

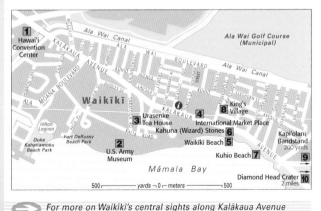

For more on Waikīkī's central sights along Kalākaua Avenue see pp20–21

1 Hawai'i Convention Center

A contemporary masterpiece of glass and soaring white columns, the Convention Center, across the Ala Wai bridge from Waikīkī proper, was dedicated in 1998 and contains dozens of artworks and more than a million square feet of meeting space. Lecture tours are held on Wednesdays and Thursdays. ⊗ *1801 Kalākaua Ave.* • *Map K6* • *943 3500 for tour info* • *8am–5pm weekdays* • *www.hawaii convention.com*

2 U.S. Army Museum

"Waikīkī's best-kept secret," this well-designed free museum celebrates the U.S. Army's many-faceted history in the Pacific. It covers Hawai'i's "Go for Broke" 100th Infantry Battalion, Waikīkī as a Vietnam War R & R center, and more. ⊗ *Battery Randolph, Kālia Road, Fort DeRussy* • *Map J7* • *438 2821* • *9am–5pm Tue–Sat* • *www.hiarmy museumsoc.org*

3 Urasenke Tea House

Teaching Cha-do, the Way of Tea, a ceremony meant to both relax and focus the mind, is the mission of this center endowed

International Market Place

by the Urasenke Organization in Kyoto. Tea ceremonies are held Wednesdays and Fridays at 10am and 11am; wear comfortable clothes (not shorts). ⊗ *245 Saratoga Rd.* • *Map J6* • *923 3059* • *Donation*

4 International Market Place

The 50+-year-old market place, originally a fanciful shopping area and cultural park, has undergone a multi-million-dollar renovation project. Expect pathways beneath spreading trees and across ponds that recall the area's illustrious past, when it was Queen Emma's garden. You will also find a performance area, a low-rise shopping and food hall, and spots for hula, artisans, and storytellers. ⊗ *2330 Kalākaua Ave.* • *Map K6*

Waikīkī Beach

Left **Kūhiō Beach** Right **Changing of the guard at King's Village**

Waikīkī Beach

This unassuming strip of white sand covered with half-clothed bodies, surfboard racks, and gawking tourists is what the beach is all about. You might think only visitors use it, but you'll see surfers, daily exercisers, canoe clubs, and other locals enjoying Hawai'i's best-known beach, too. Dawn and dusk are ideal times to visit *(see also p46.)* ⊗ Map L7

Kahuna (Wizard) Stones

The four misshapen slabs at Kūhiō Beach represent four mysterious historical figures called *Kapaemahu* ("people of a changeable nature"). These men came to Hawai'i from abroad and lived with the islanders, curing and educating them. The stones were erected in their memory and have since occupied various locations, currently gathered at the beach formerly known as Ulukou. ⊗ *Kūhiō Beach, Kalākaua Ave.* • *Map L7*

Kūhiō Beach

Once known as Hamohamo, this area was the location of Pualeilani, the beach home of Queen Kapi'olani and later her adopted son, Prince Jonah Kūhiō Kalaniana'ole, a

Waikīkī Magic

At the far western end of Waikīkī is Magic Island, a man-made green peninsula lined with walkways and ending in a sandy lagoon and rock wall popular with fishermen. End the day here, watching the soft light fall and the canoe teams ready for the next regatta. Keep an eye open for the "green flash" at sunset. Parking is free.

delegate to the U.S. Congress. During his lifetime he opened the beach near his home to the public, and left it to the city when he died. ⊗ Map L7

King's Village

This cobblestone shopping mall recreates the period of David Kalākaua, the last Hawaiian king,

Kahuna (Wizard) Stones

who ruled from 1874–91. Mock 19th-century shops sell souvenirs, clothing, and jewelry, and there are various food stalls and themed restaurants. Entertainment is provided by street artists and hula dancers. 🚫 131 Ka'iulani Ave. • Map L6 • 237 6344 • 10am–11pm daily

Kapi'olani Bandstand

The current, vaguely Victorian stone structure – a spacious circular stage with a peaked roof held up by a series of pillars – is the fourth incarnation of a bandstand first built in the 1880s. It's a popular venue for concerts and often used for informal jam sessions. 🚫 Map C7

Diamond Head Crater

Hawai'i's most-recognized landmark watches over Waikīkī, its sculpted slopes shadowy green in rainy season, parched brown at other times. In addition to the trail within the crater, a three-mile loop walk allows you to see the changeable peak from a full circle. Start where Monsarrat Avenue meets Diamond Head Road and proceed in either direction (see also pp21, 38 & 42). 🚫 Map C7

Diamond Head Crater

The Waikīkī Trail

Morning

⏰ Take a self-guided tour along the Waikīkī Historic Trail that is maintained by the Native Hawaiian Hospitality Association. Be sure to stop at each historic trail marker to learn about the area's rich history. Visit www.waikiki-historictrail.com for a free trail map.

The trail was the brainchild of the late visionary George S. Kanahele, a pioneer of cultural tourism. It's marked by a series of sculpted surfboards imprinted with photographs, maps, and information at 23 locations around the neighborhood.

Most hikers begin at the first marker on Waikīkī Beach at the site of the Outrigger Canoe Club, founded in 1908 to promote surfing, canoe paddling, and other activities.

Stopping points include a former residence of Queen Lili'uokalani; the villa of Chun Afong, who was Hawai'i's first Chinese millionaire; the vast coconut grove of Helumoa; and a war camp of Kamehameha the Great.

Late Morning

The tour lasts about an hour-and-a-half, after which you have plenty of time to stroll some more or do some shopping.

Stop for lunch at the **Hau Tree Lanai** at the east end of Waikīkī (see p74). Here you can sit right where Robert Louis Stevenson did in 1893 as he penned stories about the South Pacific.

Price Categories

Price categories include a three-course meal for one, a glass of house wine, and all unavoidable extra charges including tax.

$	under $20
$$	$20–$30
$$$	$30–$45
$$$$	$45–$60
$$$$$	over $60

Puka Dog

TOP 10 Places to Eat

Puka Dog
1 This Kauai fast-food favorite has a convenient Waikīkī location and serves fresh Polish sausages with signature relishes. A veggie version is also available. It makes for a truely Hawaiian experience. ◎ 2301 Kūhiō Ave. • Map K6 • 924 7887 • $

Wailana Coffee House
2 Reliable food and fast service draw locals and tourists to this 24-hour diner. ◎ 1860 Ala Moana Blvd. • Map H6 • 955 1764 • $

Morimoto
3 The renowned Iron Chef can sometimes be found behind the sushi bar at his namesake restaurant, in the trendy Waikīkī Edition hotel (see p117). ◎ 1775 Ala Moana Blvd. • Map G6 • 943 5900 • $$$$$

Eggs 'n' Things
4 The best place for breakfast in Waikīkī. The fresh fish, crêpes, pancakes, and waffles are worth the wait. ◎ 343 Saratoga Rd. • Map J6 • 923 3447 • 6am–2pm • $

Hula Grill Waikīkī
5 Regional Hawaiian fare is served here along the water's edge with views of the beach and Diamond Head. ◎ 2335 Kalākaua Ave. • Map K6 • 923 4852 • Breakfast, lunch & dinner • $$$

House Without a Key
6 Named after a Charlie Chan detective novel, this classic hotel hangout is a sunset favorite for those wanting a cocktail or casual meal. There is also live music and hula dancing. ◎ Halekulani Hotel, 2199 Kālia Rd. • Map J7 • 923 2311 • $$$$

Hy's Steakhouse
7 Dine here like a guest at an English mansion. Hy's is revered for its steaks, chops, and seafood, broiled over native Hawaiian kiawe wood. ◎ 2440 Kūhiō Ave. • Map L6 • 922 5555 • Dinner only • $$$$$

La Mer
8 When you're in the mood to savor each exquisite bite and watch the sun set, choose this classy French eatery. ◎ Halekulani Hotel, 2199 Kālia Rd. • Map J7 • 923 2311 • Jacket required • Dinner only • $$$$$

Wolfgang's Steakhouse
9 This upscale steakhouse in the Royal Hawaiian Center is popular with the rich and famous. The walls are adorned with photos of visiting celebs. ◎ 2301 Kalākaua Ave. • Map K6 • 922 3600 • $$$$$

Hau Tree Lanai
10 Reasonably priced East-West food is served here beneath the spreading branches of a hau tree. ◎ New Otani Kaimana Beach Hotel, 2863 Kalākaua Ave. • Map M7 • 921 7066 • Breakfast, lunch & dinner • $$$

Note: Unless otherwise stated, all restaurants accept credit cards and serve vegetarian meals

Left **Society of Seven** Right **Duke's Waikīkī**

🔟 Clubs and Shows

1 Kelly O'Neils
Punters relish O'Neils' Irish ambience, full beer and food menu, and nightly live entertainment.
Ⓢ *311 Lewers St. • Map J6 • 926 1777*

2 Chai's Island Bistro
Some of Hawaii's favorite entertainers, including the Brothers Cazimero and Jerry Santos, present the best contemporary Hawaiian music in a varied nightly schedule of performances here. Ⓢ *• Aloha Tower Marketplace • Map H4 • 585 0011*

3 Lewers Lounge
This romantic cocktail lounge has some of the island's leading mixologists and features nightly live jazz. Ⓢ *Halekulani Hotel, 2199 Kālia Road • Map J7 • 923 2311*

4 Hard Rock Café
Surfing memorabilia and rock mementoes cover the walls here, and there's live music and dancing every Friday night. Ⓢ *280 Beach Walk Ave. • Map G5 • 955 7383*

5 Hawaii Comedy Theater
Live comedy shows, featuring both local and national touring comedians, provide visitors with an affordable opportunity to laugh at the "lighter side" of the islands. Open mic nights are also held. Ⓢ *Sheraton Princess Ka'iulani Hotel, Ka'iulani Ave. • Map L6 • 531 4242*

6 Magic of Polynesia
Illusionist John Hirokawa weaves elements of Polynesian culture and "prestidigitational" puzzlement. (An understudy performs on Sun & Mon nights.)
Ⓢ *Holiday Inn Waikīkī Beachcomber, 2300 Kālākaua Ave. • Map K7 • 971 4321*

7 Society of Seven
This long-running variety show consists of show tunes, '60s hits, and costumed pratfalls. Ⓢ *Outrigger Waikīkī on the Beach, Main Showroom • Map K7 • 922 6408 • Tue–Sat*

8 Duke's Waikīkī
Named after surf legend Duke Kahanamoku and outfitted with his memorabilia, this lively bar frequented by a mixed-age crowd offers food and live music.
Ⓢ *Outrigger Waikīkī on the Beach, 2335 Kālākaua Ave. • Map K7 • 922 2268*

9 Creation, A Polynesian Journey
Polynesian music, dance, and legend make up this show.
Ⓢ *Sheraton Princess Ka'iulani, 'Ainahau Showroom, 120 Ka'iulani Ave. • Map K7 • 931 4660 • Tue & Thu–Sun*

10 Wang Chung's
This quaint, gay-friendly nightclub is a popular karaoke spot, with specialty liquors for those in need of Dutch courage.
Ⓢ *2410 Koa Ave. • Map L6 • 921 9176*

Left **Statue, Waimea** Center **Classic motor, Hale'iwa** Right **Ali'i Beach Park**

North Shore

THE NORTH SHORE IS MANY THINGS *to many people. For big wave riders, it is the peak of their craft – the navel, the source. For Honolululuans, it's the far, far country, and turning around point for Sunday drives. And for those who appreciate fresh, flavorful food, it's fast becoming an important source of superb produce, ranging from tropical fruits to coffee, corn to free-range beef. The coastline itself displays a split personality during the course of the year. From April to October, the beaches are playgrounds, broad and golden, visited by gentle waves, and smiled on by the sun. From October through March, however, high surf robs the beaches of sand, or piles it high into dunes, and the potential danger of swimming here cannot be overstated.*

🔟 Sights

1. Banzai Pipeline
2. Pūpūkea Beach Park
3. Pu'uomahuka Heiau
4. Waimea Valley Audubon Center
5. Hale'iwa Ali'i Beach Park & Hale'iwa Beach County Park
6. Hale'iwa Town
7. Queen Lili'uokalani Protestant Church
8. Waimea Bay
9. Dillingham Airfield
10. Ka'ena Point

Hale'iwa

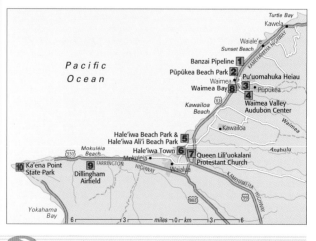

Around O'ahu – North Shore

Pu'uomahuka Heiau

This *luakini heiau* (sacrificial temple), honoring the war god Kū, is the largest on the island. It encompasses an expansive network of three enclosures that command panoramic views of Waimea Bay and the surrounding countryside. An altar has been restored at which you may see (but not touch) personal offerings.
⊗ *From Kamehameha Highway, drive up the hill on Pūpūkea Road; the dirt track into the* luakini heiau *is on the right and is marked by a visitor attraction sign* • *Map B1*

Surfers on the Banzai Pipeline

Banzai Pipeline

Banzai Beach encompasses the shoreline between Ke Waena and Ke Nui Roads off Kamehameha Highway. Here, broad expanses of sand fringe a rocky shore, over which the surf boils. The most famous of the wild surfing breaks is the tubular Banzai Pipeline, which attracts the greatest risk-taking surfers. Lifeguards are kept very busy here because of the steeply sloping ocean bottom and the irresistible allure of huge winter surf. ⊗ *Map C1*

Pūpūkea Beach Park

The 80 narrow acres of Pūpūkea Beach Park include two very popular snorkeling and skin diving areas. Shark's Cove is a rocky inlet, often used by scuba diving operators for training. Three Tables is a network of shallow coral reefs and ponds. The Pūpūkea Foodland store, across the highway, is an excellent stop for provisions, and the Sunset Beach Fire Station offers aid and information. ⊗ *Map B1*

Waimea Valley

Once an adventure park with tram rides and cliff divers, this valley is now owned by the Office of Hawaiian Affairs. The center's focus is on the conservation of the valley's natural resources and layered history through interpretive hikes and cultural activities.
⊗ *59-864 Kamehameha Hwy, Hale'iwa* • *Map C2* • *638 7766* • *www.waimea valley.net* • *Daily* • *Adm*

Waimea Valley

Sign up for DK's email newsletter on traveldk.com   77

Hale'iwa Town harbor

5 Hale'iwa Ali'i Beach Park & Hale'iwa Beach County Park

These parks flank each other on either side of the Anahulu River, and if they look familiar it's because they were a primary set for *Baywatch Hawai'i*. Ali'i Park features a boat ramp and is popular for fishing and surfing. Across the river, Hale'iwa Beach offers safe swimming and is an excellent place for a family party or picnic. ◈ *Map B2*

6 Hale'iwa Town

Plan your day to allow a couple of hours exploring historic Hale'iwa Town – the touristy top layer is built on a genuine base of community, made up of an eclectic mix of surfers, characters, and families who have lived in "the house of the 'iwa bird" for generations. Once a gracious retreat for wealthy summer visitors, the place has a certain timelessness. To get a feel for it, park at either end of town and walk, poking into shops and lingering on the Anahulu River Bridge to watch the water flow by. ◈ *Map B2*

The Wild North Shore

If you're interested in wildlife, several beaches along this coast are basking areas for turtles. Wedge-tailed shearwaters nest in the area in the late summer and fall, and whales can be seen frolicking offshore from November through April.

7 Queen Lili'uokalani Protestant Church

Queen Lili'uokalani was part of this congregation when she visited her summer home in Hale'iwa. Though the present structure dates only from 1961, a century-old moon-phase clock she gave to the church is proudly displayed. The church is famed for its annual fundraising

Queen Lili'uokalani Protestant Church

Ka'ena Point

lū'au feast each August. ✆ 66-090
Kamehameha Hwy • Map B2 • 637 9364
• Open daily

8 Waimea Bay

This legendary surf spot
is also a good choice for
scuba divers and free divers.
The wide sandy beach is perfect
for sunbathers and families.
Picnic areas, showers, and rest
rooms, make Waimea Bay an
ideal place to spend the day.
Jumping off the large rock
outcropping in the bay is
a favorite pastime among local
daredevils ✆ *Map B1 • Free*

9 Dillingham Airfield

This tiny airport is well
known as a center for gliding,
skydiving, and scenic flights
(see pp52–3). ✆ 69-000 *Farrington
Hwy, Mokulē'ia • Map A2 • 637 4551
• Honolulu Soaring (637 0207) offers
daily flights*

10 Ka'ena Point

This sprawling state park
begins at the abrupt and muddy
end of Farrington Highway and
takes you along a wild, boulder-
strewn shoreline to the dunes at
O'ahu's westernmost tip. This is
said to be where the souls of the
dead leapt into the afterlife. It's
a broiling hot 2.5-hour hike
(Ka'ena means "the heat"), but
worth it for the beauty of the landscape and the whales you can
spot in season. Take sunscreen,
water, hat, and sturdy walking
shoes. ✆ *Map A2*

North Shore Excursion

Morning

🕐 Begin with this premise:
it's too far to drive in one
day. Granted, a 50-mile
round trip from Waikīkī
may not seem like much,
but remember that most
of the route is on two-lane
highways, so you can't
rush, and there's a lot to
see. So, if possible, check
in at the **Turtle Bay
Resort** in Kahuku *(see
p117)*, which offers
hotel rooms and suites
renovated in Plantation
style, as well as condos
and cottages with full
kitchens and multiple
bedrooms.

From there, you can easily
run into **Hale'iwa** for a
morning's shopping –
there's LOTS of it and
some items are actually
cheaper than in the city,
notably pareau wraps.
Have lunch at **Kua'aina**
or **Hale'iwa Joe's
Seafood Grill** *(see p81)*.

Afternoon

For the afternoon, you can
keep going north and take
a heart-thrilling glider ride
at **Dillingham Airfield** or
rent a water bicycle from
Surf N Sea *(see p80)* in
Hale'iwa Town. Alternatively, head back toward
the resort, stopping to sun
or snorkel along the way.

Try to plan your excursion
around an event (check
www.gohawaii.com for
an events calendar).
Highly recommended
are the rare Toro Nogashi
lantern ceremony, hosted
by Hale'iwa Shingon
Mission in August, and,
of course, the winter
championship surf meets,
which aren't easy to
predict because they
are wave-dependent.

Around O'ahu – North Shore

Left **The Growing Keiki** Center **Jungle Gems** Right **Surf & Sea**

Shops in Hale'iwa

1 Surf N Sea
This watersports-fanatics' paradise, the oldest surf shop on O'ahu, offers everything from swimwear to snorkel tours and kayak rentals. The friendly staff will even fix that ding in your board after you've tackled Waimea Bay. ✆ *62-595 Kamehameha Hwy, Hale'iwa • 637 9887*

2 The Growing Keiki
If there's a young one on your travel gift list, check out this eclectic array of funky children's clothing, books, toys, and gifts. ✆ *66-051 Kamehameha Hwy, Hale'iwa • 637 4544*

3 North Shore Swimwear
This specializes in original bathing suit designs, ranging from thongs to tanks and in sizes from tiny to large. Bottoms and tops are sold separately so you can always get the right fit. ✆ *66-250 Kamehameha Hwy, Hale'iwa • 637 7000*

4 Strong Current Surf Design
Longboard specialists with a major sideline in T-shirts. It's hung floor to ceiling with '60s surf memorabilia. ✆ *66-214 Kamehameha Hwy, Hale'iwa • 637 3410*

5 Polynesian Treasures
Stacked with unusual designs by more than 50 artisans. Check out carved bone amulets, quilted items, and cool purses. ✆ *North Shore Marketplace, Hale'iwa • 637 1288*

6 Silver Moon Emporium
You'll think you're in SoHo or Hollywood when you step into this ritzy boutique packed with designer clothes and shoes of the wispy, whimsical type. This is where the movie, TV, and sports stars shop when they visit the North Shore. ✆ *North Shore Marketplace, Hale'iwa • 637 7710*

7 Jungle Gems
Step into a world of incense and stone and lose yourself in eye-popping displays of crystals and polished beads, gold and silver jewelry, and samples of Hawaiian minerals. ✆ *North Shore Marketplace, Hale'iwa • 637 6609*

8 Barnfield's Raging Isle Surf and Cycle
Everything for bicycles, including rentals and repairs. You'll also find custom boards by Bill Barnfield and stylish casual wear. ✆ *North Shore Marketplace, Hale'iwa • 637 7707*

9 Britton Gallery
Always on the lookout for handmade and original artworks, this shop features woodwork, jewelry, paintings, and sculptures by some 35 Hawai'i artists. ✆ *North Shore Marketplace, Hale'iwa • 637 6505*

10 Hale'iwa Art Gallery
George Atkins' gallery has original works by more than 30 Pacific Island artists, ranging from the neo-realism of Mark Cross to the abstracts of Mihoko M. ✆ *66-252 Kamehameha Hwy, Hale'iwa • 637 3368*

Left **Coffee Gallery** Right **Kua 'Aina Sandwich Shop**

Price categories include a three-course meal for one, a glass of house wine, and all unavoidable extra charges including tax.	**$**	under $20
	$$	$20–$30
	$$$	$30–$45
	$$$$	$45–$60
	$$$$$	over $60

Around O'ahu – North Shore

🔟 Places to Eat in Hale'iwa

1 Ted's Bakery
The source of heavenly cream pies sold all over the island; the chocolate-*haupia* (coconut) is Ted's signature. Stop by from 7am to pick up fresh pastries and coffee. ◈ *59-024 Kamehameha Hwy, Hale'iwa • 638 8207 • $*

2 Waialua Bakery
A popular hangout with surfers. The excellent smoothies, sandwiches, and cookies keep visitors coming back for more. ◈ *66-200 Kamehameha Hwy, Hale'iwa • 637 9079 • $*

3 Jameson's by the Sea
This longtime favorite steak and seafood restaurant has a gallery and gift shop, too. ◈ *62-540 Kamehameha Hwy, Hale'iwa • 637 6262 • $$$$*

4 Hale'iwa Joe's Seafood Grill
With a view of Hale'iwa harbor from its patio, the restaurant specializes in "boat drinks" and fresh fish. ◈ *66-011 Kamehameha Hwy, Hale'iwa • 637 8005 • $$$*

5 Shave Ice Stops
Two neighboring operations specialize in sweet, drippy shave ice. This treat is a legacy of the days when ice was shipped to Hawai'i from Alaska in giant blocks. The shavings, created when the blocks were cut, were treasured by children. In the 1920s, Chinese entrepreneurs created fruit syrups to pour over the ice, and Japanese craftsmen created a plane-like device to shave it. Latch on to the shortest line and enjoy. ◈ *Matsumoto's (66-087 K. Hwy) • Aoki's (66-117 K. Hwy)*

6 Pizza Bob's
Pies, salads, and sandwiches, as well as pizzas. ◈ *66-145 Kamehameha Hwy, Hale'iwa • 637 5095 • $$*

7 Luibueno's Mexican Seafood & Fish Market
This restaurant, bar, and fish market is a local favorite for its traditional Baja-style Mexican food made using fresh local ingredients. ◈ *66-165 Kamehameha Hwy, Hale'iwa • 637 7717 • $$$*

8 Kua'aina Sandwich Shop
Famous for its third-of-a-pound burgers and crisp fries. Look for the crowd just off the highway near the end of town. ◈ *66-160 Kamehameha Hwy, Hale'iwa • 637 6067 • $$*

9 Coffee Gallery
Locally grown coffees are roasted daily at this Internet café. ◈ *North Shore Marketplace, Hale'iwa • 637 5571 • $$*

10 Café Hale'iwa
Ample, cheap breakfasts and Mexican-accented lunches are the fare here; they're open only until mid-afternoon. A popular surfer hangout, it's good for people-watching and finding out what's on in town. ◈ *66-460 Kamehameha Hwy, Hale'iwa • 637 5516 • $$*

Note: Unless otherwise stated, all restaurants accept credit cards and serve vegetarian meals

Left **Dole Plantation** Center **Canoes on Mākaha Beach** Right **Hawai'i Plantation Village**

Central & Leeward O'ahu

FOR VISITORS WHO HAVE THE TIME to venture beyond the fleshpots of Waikīkī and the allure of the North Shore, Central and Leeward O'ahu offer the chance to better understand the everyday life of the island – the neighborhoods and shops, the down home restaurants, the lesser known beaches, and historic sites. 'Ewa, once the quintessential company town, recalls its roots with a reconstruction plantation village. The second city of Kapolei has the state's only water park, while Ko Olina's gentle lagoons and the beaches of Wai'anae offer great sun and sand time. Several sacred sites – some restored, some mere remnants – remind us of the historical importance of these areas.

🔟 Sights

1. Hawai'i Plantation Village
2. Kukaniloko Birthing Stones
3. Dole Plantation
4. Wet 'n' Wild Hawaii
5. Hawaiian Railway Line
6. Pōka'i Bay
7. Kū'ilioloa Heiau
8. Mākaha Beach
9. Kāne'aki Heiau
10. Yokohama Bay

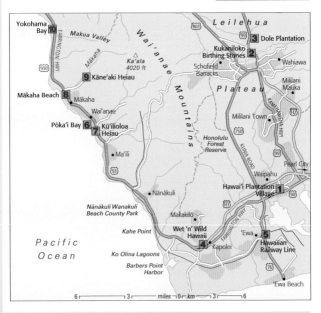

Previous pages **Byodo-in Temple** (see p24)

Kukaniloko Birthing Stones

1 Hawai'i Plantation Village

The era when more than 400,000 immigrants and Hawaiians labored on sugar and pineapple plantations is memorialized in the 30 original structures gathered to create this living history museum. Tours are led by volunteers, many of whom are former plantation laborers or descendants of workers. 🌀 *94-695 Waipahu Street, Waipahu • Map C4 • 677 0110 • 10am–4:30pm Mon–Sat • www. hawaiiplantationvillage.org • Adm age 4+*

2 Kukaniloko Birthing Stones

Bloodlines were all-important to ancient Hawaiians. In royal birthing areas like this, the upright stones served as support for the chiefly mother and also as chairs for the attendant priests and relatives, on hand to testify to the child's lineage. 🌀 *From Kamehameha Hwy heading toward Wahiawā, turn left on Whitmore Rd., continue to dirt parking lot, and palm grove • Map C3*

3 Dole Plantation

The gardens and production facilities of this popular attraction introduce 900,000 visitors a year to O'ahu's modern-day diversified agriculture industry. The pineapple is familiar, but also growing here are coffee, tropical fruit, corn, *lei* flowers, and exotic bromeliads. The Pineapple Garden maze, officially recognized in the Guinness Book of Records as the world's largest maze, offers an unusual diversion. 🌀 *64-1550 Kamehameha Hwy • Map C3 • 621 8408 • 9am–5:30pm daily • www.dole-plantation.com*

4 Wet 'n' Wild Hawaii

As if the miles of beaches aren't enough, this inland water park forms another attraction, especially for children. They just can't get enough of the tube cruises, six-story speed slide, beach volleyball, and special birthday area. 🌀 *400 Farrington Hwy, Kapolei (exit 1 off H1) • Map B5 • 674 9283 • Jun–Aug: daily; Sep–May: Thu–Mon • www.wetnwildhawaii.com • Adm*

The water park at Wet 'n' Wild Hawaii

For Pearl Harbor see pp8–9

5 Hawaiian Railway Line

The Hawaiian Railway Line is six restored miles of what were once 70-plus miles of track delivering people and supplies from 'Ewa to Honolulu. It operates Sundays, offering 90-minute round trips to the

Ko Olina's lagoons

coast at Ko Olina and back. Take the train, then later drive back to Ko Olina to swim in the man-made lagoons in the shade of coco-palms. You can also have lunch or dinner at the JW Marriott 'Ihilani Resort & Spa *(see Azul, p89)*. Ⓢ Catch the train from 91-1001 Renton Road, 'Ewa • Map C5 • 681 5461 • www.hawaiianrailway.com • Fare

Ka'ena from the West

Though most folks come to Ka'ena Point from the Mokulē'ia side, the 5-mile trek from the Wai'anae direction offers a sandier section of the old Farrington Highway. En route, watch for yellow *'ilima*, purple *pā'ū o hi'iaka* and white *naupaka* flowers.

6 Pōka'i Bay

Beautiful, tranquil Pōka'i Beach County Park is the most welcoming swimming and snorkeling beach along the Wai'anae Coast. It's safe year round because of the protection of a long breakwater. The bay's name, "night of the great one," is rooted in the story of a voyager from the south, Pōka'i, who is said to have planted the first coconut grove on the island on this site. Ⓢ 85-037 Wai'anae Valley Rd. • Map A4

Mākaha Beach

7 Kū'ilioloa Heiau

This sacred site on Kāne'ilio Point is believed to have been a blessing point for travelers arriving and departing by canoe. Its name refers to a dog-god who protected voyagers. Ⓢ Map A4

Pōka'i Bay

Mākaha Beach

Mākaha ("fierce" in Hawaiian) lives up to its name, with high surf and a runoff pond behind the beach that periodically breaks through the sand bar and rushes into the bay. In the old days, it was infamous for a group of bandits who terrorized the area. Today, with the exception of when the surf is high, this is a safe beach for swimming.

Ⓝ *84-369 Farrington Hwy • Map A3*

Kāne'ākī Heiau

Located in a lush, park-like setting at the back of Mākaha Valley, this superbly preserved and restored sacred site was once a benign agricultural temple for the god Lono. It became a *luakini* (temple of human sacrifice) when Kamehameha I used the area as a gathering point for his troops while preparing for battle with Kaua'i.

Ⓝ *Located inside the gated Mauna'olu Estates (request entry at the gate) • Map A3 • 695 8174 • 10am–2pm Tue–Sun*

Yokohama Bay

So-called because of its popularity with Japanese pole fishermen, this is the last sandy shore on the northwestern coast of O'ahu. It's also part of a large but undeveloped park complex that stretches around the end of the island to Ka'ena. Though known as a popular surfing site, it is also a place where you can enjoy the beach in relative isolation. Ⓝ *Map A3*

Surfer, Yokohama Bay

A Day with Dolphins

Morning

🕐 Schools of spinner and bottlenose dolphins, and, from November to March, pods of humpback whales are readily seen just off the **Wai'anae Coast**. Several cruise companies offer dolphin-watching excursions in various craft, usually with small numbers of passengers. The excursions depart from **Wai'anae Boat Harbor** or **Ko Olina Marina**. Most offer transport from Waikīkī hotels, though you can choose to pick up the tour at the harbor. You will have to get up early, because the boats usually depart promptly at 7am.

Wild Side Specialty Tours (www.sailhawaii.com, 306 7273) offers a whale- and dolphin-watching cruise aboard a 42-foot catamaran. It is operated by marine researchers who believe that sail-powered vessels are less disruptive to the animals. The boat accommodates an intimate 4 to 15 passengers and the four-hour morning excursions include refreshments.

Afternoon

🍴 For a Mediterranean-style lunch after your cruise, try **Azul** in Ko Olina *(see p89)*.

If you're traveling with kids who want to emulate the dolphins, you can spend the rest of the day at **Wet 'n' Wild Hawaii** *(see p85)*. Less energetic members of the party can relax in the café or lie in shallow water away from the screaming action.

Left **Blaisdell Park** Center **Aloha Stadium** Right **Wahiawā Botanical Gardens**

🔟 Best of the Rest

1 Blaisdell Park
On the shore of Pearl Harbor, Blaisdell is a family favorite due to its pavilion facilities, shade trees, and children's play equipment. ⚑ 98-319 Kamehameha Hwy, Pearl City • Map C4 • Free

2 Aloha Stadium Swap Meet
Ringed around the coliseum-like stadium, the largest swap meet in the islands is a great place for kitsch souvenirs, alohawear, and beach equipment. ⚑ 99-500 Salt Lake Blvd. • Map D4 • 486 6704 • 8am–3pm Wed & Sat, 6:30am–3pm Sun

3 Waipahu Town
This one-time plantation town is the hub for O'ahu's Filipino community. Activities at the Filcom Center (94-428 Makuola St.), the largest Filipino community center outside of the Philippines, include dance and martial-arts classes and film screenings. ⚑ Map C4

4 Waikele Premium Outlets
This vast outlet mall includes factory-direct shops for Sak's Fifth Avenue and Coach, as well as Banana Republic, Calvin Klein, Levi's, Juicy Couture, and Tommy Hilfiger. ⚑ 94-790 Lumiana St., Waipahu, Exit 5A off H1 • Map C4 • 676 5656

5 Wahiawā Town
Primarily a military town, dusty Wahiawā, high on the central plain, is an unglamorous but useful stop-off for supplies when journeying through the hinterland. ⚑ Map C3

6 Wahiawā Botanical Gardens
Founded by commercial planters as an experimental garden, this 25-acre arboretum encompasses a tropical rain forest and upland gardens. ⚑ 1396 California Ave., Wahiawā • Map C3 • 621 5463 • 9am–4pm daily • Free

7 Don Quijote
This Japanese discount store is open 24 hours, making it a convenient stop for groceries, inexpensive souvenirs, and other essentials. ⚑ 94-144 Farringdon Hwy, Waipahu • Map C4 • 678 6800

8 Pearlridge Shopping Center
This two-section shopping mall (connected by a monorail) is especially popular with tweens and teens. ⚑ 98-1005 Moanalua Rd., 'Aiea • Map D4 • 488 0981

9 'Aiea Bowl
This bustling bowling alley is a family-friendly spot by day, with many dining options, but things liven up at night, with glow-in-the-dark "cosmic bowling" and dancing until 2am. ⚑ 99-115 'Aiea Heights Dr. • Map D4 • 488 6854

10 Ice Palace
O'ahu's full service ice rink is open daily for public skating and is a perfect escape from the heat. Skate rental is included in the admission price. ⚑ 4510 Salt Lake Blvd. • Map D4 • 487 9921 • Adm

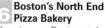

Price Categories

Price categories include a three-course meal for one, a glass of house wine, and all unavoidable extra charges including tax.

$	under $20
$$	$20–$30
$$$	$30–$45
$$$$	$45–$60
$$$$$	over $60

Left **Azul** Right **Boston's North End Pizza Bakery**

TOP 10 Places to Eat

1 Buzz's Original Steak House, 'Aiea

A longtime local favorite, Buzz's is known for its generous salad bar, grilled steaks, and fresh seafood. The original "Original" is in Kailua. *98-751 Kuahou Pl., 'Aiea, Pearl City • Map D4 • 487 6465 • $$$*

2 Champa Thai

Award-winning Thai spot, with a dozen types of curry and an expansive vegetarian menu. *Pearl Kai Shopping Center, 98-199 Kamehameha Hwy, 'Aiea • Map D4 • 488 2881 • $$*

3 Molly's Smokehouse

This rare source of Texas-style barbecue is widely patronized by southerners from nearby military bases. *23 S. Kamehameha Hwy, Suite No. 102, Wahiawā • Map C3 • 621 4858 • $$*

4 Shiro's Saimin Haven & Family Restaurant

This shrine to Japanese-style noodle soup and immense local plate lunches has to be seen to be believed. Founder and patriarch Shiro Matsuo has lined the walls with scribbled notes expressing his philosophy of life. *Waimalu Shopping Center, 98-020 Kamehameha Hwy, 'Aiea • Map D5 • 488 8824 • $*

5 Anna Miller's

Known for its homemade pies and friendly staff, this popular family restaurant will serve you breakfast, lunch, or dinner 24 hours a day. *98-115 Kaonohi St., 'Aiea • Map D4 • 487 2421 • $$*

6 Boston's North End Pizza Bakery

The pies are Boston-style – thick edge, thin center, cheesy, saucy – and the attitude is East Coast too. That means "eat it and beat it." *98-298 Kamehameha Hwy, 'Aiea • Map D4 • 487 4055 • $*

7 Azul

This fine dining restaurant at the JW Marriott 'Ihilani Resort & Spa *(see p117)* is a lovely, shady and cool space, opening onto a tropical lagoon. The Mediterranean menu manages to be both refined and rustic. *92-101 Olani St., Ko Olina • Map B5 • 679 0079 • $$$$*

8 Roy's Ko Olina

Award-winning chef and restaurateur Roy Yamaguchi perfects his Hawai'i fusion cuisine, while bringing the excitement of the open-plan kitchen to the islands. *92-110 Aliinui Dr., Ko Olina Golf Club • Map B5 • 676 7697 • $$$$*

9 Ushio-Tei

This quiet oasis in the JW Marriott 'Ihilani Resort & Spa *(see p117)* serves traditional Japanese fare and has a popular all-you-can-eat buffet. *92-1001 Olani St., Ko Olina • Map B5 • 679 0079 • $$$*

10 Wai'anae Chop Suey

More Chinese cuisine in typical island style – from egg flower soup, and lemon chicken to sweet & sour spare ribs, and deep-fried whole fish. *Wai'anae Mall Shopping Center • Map A4 • 696 1888 • $$*

Note: *Unless otherwise stated, all restaurants accept credit cards and serve vegetarian meals*

Left **Fishpond, He'eia State Park** Center **Canoes, Kailua Beach** Right **Riding at Kualoa Ranch**

Windward O'ahu

FROM KAILUA TO KAHUKU IS A JOURNEY *from town to country, suburb to rural O'ahu. Kailua, a bedroom community of Honolulu, is an upscale neighborhood of beach and lake homes, while Kāne'ohe accommodates a Marine base and Hawaiian homestead lands. North from Kāne'ohe, the route along Kamehameha Highway passes a string of sandy beaches and brooding valleys, watched over by the sharp-etched Ko'olau Mountain Range.*

Left **Mokoli'i Island** Right **Camping, Kualoa Regional Park**

🔟 Sights

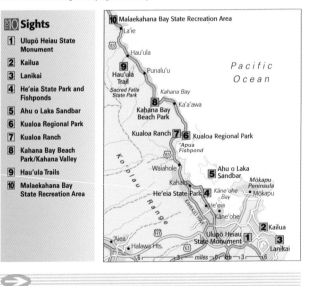

Lava rock at Ulupō Heiau State Monument

interesting gift and clothing shops, and at number 600 Lanikai Juice, which serves smoothies and juices. ◈ *Map F4*

3 Lanikai

Developed as a beach retreat in the 1920s, Lanikai (reached by a beach road south of Kailua) is one of the most sought-after addresses on O'ahu. The neighborhood remains tight-knit, hosting community plays and an exceptional pre-Christmas craft fair. ◈ *Map F4*

1 Ulupō Heiau State Monument

Some still arrange leaf-wrapped gift bundles on the massive rock platform, once a site of prayer, sacrifice, ceremony, and divina-tion. Likely built during the time of Kamehameha I, the *heiau* con-tinued in use until the ancient religion was officially abandoned. If Kailua-bound on Highway 61, turn left into Ulu'oa Street at the Windward YMCA, park in the Y lot or along the street and follow the signs. ◈ *Map E4*

2 Kailua

This country-chic town con-sists of a few blocks of shops and restaurants, peaceful '60s-era neighborhoods, and a string of popular beaches. Park along Kailua Road and explore on foot to find

4 He'eia State Park and Fishponds

North on Kamehameha Highway from Kāne'ohe, surrounded by mangrove swamp, this grassy, well-maintained state park offers a view of the 80-acre He'eia fishpond, the largest intact aqua-culture zone in the islands. When in use, fingerlings of the prized *'ama'ama* (mullet) and *'ahole* (Hawaiian flagtail) would swim into the rock-walled ponds through vertical gates called *kahala*, but would be unable to swim out. In this way, the fish were success-fully farmed. ◈ *Map E4*

The beach at Kailua

➤ For more on the beautiful Kane'ohe District **see pp24–25**; for the Polynesian Cultural Center **see pp26–27**

Kualoa Regional Park

Ahu o Laka Sandbar

At low tide on a weekend, drive slowly on Kamehameha Highway just past He'eia Kea Boat Harbor. A little way offshore, you'll see watercraft of every description clustered around seemingly nothing at all. In fact, just above sea level is a sandbar, and locals like to fetch up here, light the hibachi and hang out. Rent a canoe or kayak and join them. ◎ Map E3

The beach at Kualoa Regional Park

Shrimp Trucks

Northbound on Kamehameha Highway between Kāne'ohe and Kahuku, you'll encounter a string of shrimp trucks, some in lunchwagons, others in roadside stands. It all began with a single shrimp aquaculture operation, which sparked a North Shore love affair with crustaceans. If you stop, be sure to ask if the shrimp you're getting are locally grown (some aren't) or previously frozen.

Kualoa Regional Park

This flat, windy park, with its narrow sandy beach and shallow inshore ponds, is fantastic for kite-flying, snorkeling, launching watercraft, picnicking, and camping (by permit). The clearly visible peak sitting on the ocean (sometimes known as the China-man's Hat) is the island of Mokoli'i *(see also p25)*. ◎ Map E3

Kualoa Ranch

The valley and rolling hillsides of Kualoa were once a sacred place of refuge, then passed to missionary descendants from royal hands. Today, it is a working cattle ranch, as well as a park where visitors can enjoy equestrian experiences and movie tours *(see also p43)*. The ranch is a popular filming spot, appearing in movies and TV shows such as *Jurassic Park* and *Lost*. ◎ *Kualoa Ranch and Activity Club, 49-560 Kamehameha Hwy • Map E3 • 237 7321*

Kahana Bay Beach Park/Kahana Valley

This deep, green valley is state-owned watershed land, fronted by an eight-acre city and county park. The park has a sandy beach, bathrooms, picnic tables, lots of chickens (escaped fowl are ubiquitous all along this coast) and the remnants of two fishponds.

Kualoa Ranch

Watch for fishermen wading out to catch akule (big-eyed scad).
⊗ *Kualoa Ranch and Activity Club, Kamehameha Hwy • Map D2 • 237 7321*

9 Hau'ula Trails

Hau'ula ("red *hau* tree") is the starting point for three easy to moderate rambles. (A fourth hike, Sacred Falls is closed indefinitely due to landslide danger.) The two most worthwhile treks are Ma'akua Loop and Ma'akua Ridge (aka Papali Trail); both offer good views, interesting plants, and guavas in their late summer and fall season. ⊗ *From Kamehameha (Highway 83), the trails are reached by Hau'ula Homestead Road and Ma'akua Road • Map D2*

10 Malaekahana Bay State Recreation Area

This mile-and-a-bit of curving sandy beach is distinguished by bare-bones beach homes available for rent, a reef that keeps the inshore waters calm, and Goat Island, a wild and beautiful place that can be reached on foot at low tide; be sure to wear beach shoes. ⊗ *Map D1*

Hau'ula Trail sign

A Day on the Windward Coast

Morning

🕐 Begin your itinerary by heading straight for **Kailua**, where you can stop off at Agnes Bakery for coffee and *malassadas* (Portuguese hole-less doughnuts fried up fresh and eaten hot).

Treat yourself to some Hawaiian scents and lotions at Lanikai Bath and Body. If you're feeling peckish, pick up a sandwich at Brent's Deli (629A Kaha St), the only place resembling a true Jewish-style deli on the island.

Then it's time to head for **Kailua Beach** or **Lanikai** for a beach afternoon.

Afternoon

You could opt for a lazy, sun-soaked afternoon. But if you fancy a little more activity, rent some form of watercraft from Bob Twogood Kayaks (262 5656) or Kailua Sailboards and Kayaks (262 2555). Then, either paddle out to the **Nā Mokulua** ("the mokes" *see p47*) off Kailua Beach or drive over to He'eia Kai Boat Harbor to check out the **Ahu O Laka** sandbar.

If you do plan to spend more time on the coast, consider reserving one of the luxurious rooms at the **Turtle Bay Resort** (57-091 Kamehameha Highway, Kahuku, 293 8811). You can putter your way from Kailua to Kahuku, leaving mid-afternoon and making one or two stops, and still arrive by check-in time. You won't have to face the long drive back across the island, and you can dine in the extraordinary **21 Degrees North** *(p95)*.

Left **Under a Hula Moon** Right **Kim Taylor Reece Gallery**

ⓘ10 Places to Shop

1 Under a Hula Moon
Delightful, Hawaiian-themed furnishings for kitchen and bedroom – particularly a child's room, with toys and sweet little tea sets. ⓢ *600 Kailua Road, Kailua Shopping Center • Map F4 • 261 4252*

2 Bookends in Kailua
This stacked-high bookshop is a rare find in Hawai'i: a place run by readers for readers, with comfy chairs and a mix of used books and new titles. A great supply of locally published works, too. ⓢ *590 Kailua Road, Kailua Shopping Center • Map F4 • 261 1996*

3 Island Treasures Art Gallery
Kailua Koa wood craft, *lauhala* (woven pandanus) creations, and ceramics are among the treasures for sale here, alongside works by local artists. ⓢ *629 Kailua Road, Kailua Shopping Center • Map F4 • 261 8131*

4 Jeff Chang Pottery & Fine Crafts
Jeff Chang sells his own work along with well-selected gifts, from jewelry to tabletop water fountains. ⓢ *539 Kailua Rd., Kāne'ohe • Map E4 • 262 4060*

5 The Gallery of Lance Fairly
Lance Fairly's other-worldly seascapes and landscapes glow from the canvas. In contrast, his plein-air work vividly recalls the local coastline. Originals and prints are available. ⓢ *53-839 Kamehameha Hwy, Hau'ula • Map D2 • 293 9009*

6 Kahaunani Woods & Krafts
This small roadside stand owned by Tats and Leo Enos offers original-design koa baby rattles, wine bottle holders, stir-fry spoons, and all manner of gifts made from native woods, including *koa, hau* and *milo*. ⓢ *53-850 Kamehameha Hwy, Hau'ula • Map D2*

7 Kim Taylor Reece Gallery
Reece's photographs portray alluring hula dancers in traditional dress. Hand-printed sepia originals, posters, and Reece's books are all available. ⓢ *53-866 Kamehameha Hwy, Hau'ula • Mon–Wed afternoons only • Map D2 • 293 2000*

8 Global Village
This family-owned business began as a bead store, but now also sells clothing for children and adults, jewelry, gifts, and accessories. They also hold bead workshops. ⓢ *539 Kailua Rd., Kailua • Map E4 • 262 8183*

9 Only Show in Town
Antiques and collectibles from all eras in Hawai'i history, as well as a beguiling miscellany of other times and places. ⓢ *56-901 Kamehameha Hwy, Kahuku • Map D1 • 293 1295*

10 S. Tanaka Plantation Store
Garishly repainted in a style that might shock the original owners, this plantation-era general store is now a small antiques and collectibles mall. ⓢ *56-901 Kamehameha Hwy, Kahuku • Map D1*

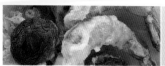

Price Categories

Price categories include a three-course meal for one, a glass of house wine, and all unavoidable extra charges including tax.

$	under $20
$$	$20–$30
$$$	$30–$45
$$$$	$45–$60
$$$$$	over $60

Shrimp tempura, Maliko O Punalu'u Bar & Grill

TOP 10 Places to Eat

1 Buzz's Original Steak House
This venerable spot – a warren of dim rooms scented with the delicious aroma of grilling meat – turns out surf and turf for everyone from Lanikai millionaires to sandy surfers. ✆ 413 Kawailoa Road, Lanikai • Map F4 • 261 4661 • $$$

2 Ola
Located right on the beach, Ola draws diners from neighboring Turtle Bay Resort for its stunning ocean views and fresh, locally inspired cuisine. ✆ 57-091 Kamehameha Hwy, Kahuku • Map C1 • 293 0801 • $$$

3 Lucy's Grill & Bar
A truly Pacific Rim restaurant, Lucy's offers well-prepared East-West dishes in a vibrant atmosphere. It has a lively bar, too, with a patio area – the only quiet place to talk. ✆ 33 Aulike Street, Kailua • Map F4 • 230 8188 • $$$$

4 Aunty Pat's Paniolo Café
Named for a descendant of the Kualoa Ranch's founder, this casual café serves breakfasts and lunches, including gourmet burgers made fresh from the ranch's herd. ✆ Kualoa Ranch, 49-560 Kamehameha Hwy • Map E3 • 237 7321 • $

5 Pah Ke's Chinese Restaurant
Besides the chop suey standards, Pah Ke's specials include chilled fruit soups and dishes that focus on locally grown tropical fruits. ✆ 46-018 Kamehameha Hwy, Kāne'ohe • Map E4 • 235 4505 • $

6 Hale'iwa Joe's
Call to check Joe's isn't reserved for a wedding – neighboring Ha'ikū Gardens does a booming bride-and-groom business. If open, expect steaks, seafood, and sandwiches. ✆ 46-336 Ha'ikū Rd., Kāne'ohe • Map E4 • 247 6671 • $$$

7 Boots & Kimo's Homestyle Kitchen
Popular with locals and tourists, this welcoming café often has lengthy lines for its delicious macadamia nut pancakes and Portuguese sausage. ✆ 151 Hekili St., Kailua • Map F4 • 263 7929 • $

8 Maliko O Punalu'u Bar & Grill
At this funky roadhouse the key ingredient is shrimp – steamed, tempura, and scampi-style. Lively bar at night. ✆ 53-146 Kamehameha Hwy, Hau'ula • Map D2 • 237 8474 • $

9 Crouching Lion Inn
Named after a nearby lion-like rock formation, this old-fashioned restaurant ladles out soups, salads, and its specialties: Slavonic Steak and Mile High Pie. ✆ 51-666 Kamehameha Hwy, Ka'a'awa • Map D2 • 237 8981 • $$$

10 21 Degrees North
Without question, the best evening dining on this side of the island. The East-West food is genuinely innovative and focuses on fresh, seasonal ingredients. ✆ Turtle Bay Resort, 57-091 Kamehameha Hwy • Map C1 • 293 8811 • $$$$$

> **Note:** Unless otherwise stated, all restaurants accept credit cards and serve vegetarian meals

Left **Hanauma Bay** Right **Waimānalo**

South Shore

I'T'S AN EASY HOUR'S DRIVE *around the South Shore of O'ahu from Waikīkī to the rural village of Waimānalo. But in the course of those dozen miles, you experience the multi-dimensional nature of an island whose Hawaiian name means "the gathering place." Beginning with the exclusive bedroom community of Kāhala, you next come to a series of densely populated, valley neighborhoods. Each of these climbs from a coral-fringed beach to the apex of a deep valley in the classic Hawaiian land division known as an* ahupua'a *(see p11). At the island's edge, the wave- and wind-tossed coast provides an ecologically fragile landscape, before giving way to mile upon mile of golden sand, bordering the horse country.*

🔟 Sights

1. Kāhala Beach
2. Paikō Lagoon State Reserve
3. Kuli'ou'ou Beach Park
4. Maunalua Bay Beach Park
5. Hanauma Bay
6. Sandy Beach
7. Makapu'u Beach Park
8. Waimānalo Bay State Recreation Area
9. Bellows Field Beach County Park
10. Waimānalo Polo Field

Sandy Beach

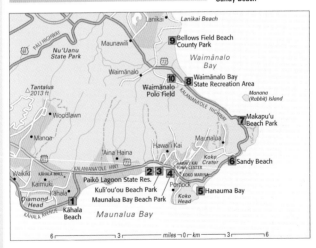

Kāhala Beach

Kāhala Beach

1 This secretive mile and a half of golden sand, hidden by the ritzy homes of suburban Kāhala, offers wading, snorkeling, reef-fishing, and sunbathing. To get here from Waikīkī, take Diamond Head Road until it becomes Kāhala Avenue. In the 4,400 to 4,800 blocks of Kāhala Avenue, watch out for seven narrow paths, marked by blue beach access signs (you'll need to park on the street). The bigger stretch of Wai'alae Beach Park (with restrooms and picnic tables) is just beyond Kapakahi Stream bridge. ◎ Map E6

Paikō Lagoon State Reserve

2 Its name deriving from a Portuguese former resident called

Maunalua Bay Beach Park

Pico, the virtually unknown Paikō Peninsula offers birdwatching, fishing, snorkeling, and unprecedented seclusion. From Kalaniana'ole, turn right onto narrow Paikō Drive, park on the street and take the beach access trail to the water. Turn left (east) and find your spot past the second to last house. You'll need to bring food and water with you, as it's a remote area. ◎ Map F5

Kuli'ou'ou Beach Park

3 This family-friendly park on Maunalua Bay offers perfect picnic sites, restrooms, views and, at low tide, the opportunity for novice kayakers to take to the water. From Kalaniana'ole, turn right on Kuli'ou'ou Road, left on Summer Street and right again on Bay, which comes to a dead end in a parking lot. ◎ Map F6

Maunalua Bay Beach Park

4 This sun-baked park has picnic tables, restrooms, and some grassy areas for play. It's a launching point for excursions onto Maunalua Bay, from outrigger canoe paddling and water skiing to fishing, diving, and snorkeling trips. ◎ Map F6

5 Hanauma Bay

Keyhole-shaped Hanauma Bay is one of the most spectacular sights in the islands, and highly recommended for swimming and snorkeling. It's a good idea to go early in the day because the bay is so well used that access and parking can be difficult. Call ahead on 396 4229 to check for periodic closures. ⊗ Map F6

6 Sandy Beach

Renowned for the constant winds that make kite-flying a feature, Sandy Beach also has wicked waves, which routinely slam unsuspecting waders and body surfers into the rock-hard sand. This much-used beach is, therefore, one to treat with respect. So rule number one is: don't turn your back on the ocean – here or anywhere else, for that matter. ⊗ Map F5

Hanauma Bay

"baby beach," where pools are safe for children's play. Manana – better known as Rabbit Island – is a dramatic landmark offshore. ⊗ Map F5

7 Makapu'u Beach Park

This park contains some of O'ahu's beloved landmarks – the beach (a bodysurfer's mecca), the nearby lighthouse, and the shore trail. Just over the rocks is

8 Waimānalo Bay State Recreation Area

Here you catch sight of uninterrupted white sand that stretches three miles along the coast. The facility includes Waimānalo Beach

Makapu'u Beach Park

For more about the coastline from Hanauma Bay to Sandy Beach see pp22–23

Kite Flying

On any windy day at Sandy Beach, the sky is bright with kites. Flyers from age 6 to 60 play out the lines, straining against the wind. Traditionally, Hawaiian kites were made from hau wood, covered with kappa or woven lauhala, with olona cord used for the string. Skill was needed both to make and fly them.

Park, south of town, and the recreation area to the north. Both offer prime picnic areas, camp sites, restrooms, and showers. The park is right on the road but the recreation area is secluded in an ironwood grove (known as Sherwood Forest, alas, in part because car burglaries are a problem). ◈ Map F5

Bellows Field Beach County Park

Though located on a military installation that includes an army reserve camp, an area where Marines practice amphibious landings, this sprawling beach and campsite with ample parking is a public facility on weekends and holidays. Many consider it the best of the Waimānalo beaches; bodyboarding, boogieboarding, and surfing are prime. Camping here is by permit only. ◈ Map F4

Waimānalo Polo Field

Polo, favored by Hawaiian royalty, has a 200-year history here. Honolulu Polo Club matches are held at 2:30pm each Sunday from June through October (adults $3, children under 12 free). There is a shaded grandstand, food for sale, and you'll find lots of aloha (warmth) for visitors – who have included the UK's Prince Charles, who played a match here in 1974. ◈ Map F5

South Shore Tour

Morning

A South Shore circular driving tour makes for a wonderful all-day itinerary. From Waikīkī, take H1 to the Wai'alae exit and start the morning with croissants at the Patisserie and shopping at **Kāhala Mall**; shorts and sandals are just fine even at this ritzy mall.

Continue south, and finish off the morning with a water adventure at **Maunalua Bay** (see p97), such as water-skiing or diving. (Reserve ahead at water activity shops at Hawai'i Kai Towne Center or Koko Marina Center.) Alternatively, for a more sedate pursuit, take the binoculars and go birdwatching on the edge of the **Paikō Lagoon State Reserve** (p97).

Back on Kalaniana'ole, grab a quick lunch at **Kona Brewing Co.** (p101) or one of a dozen inexpensive, interesting eateries at **Koko Marina Center** (p100).

Afternoon

Cruise slowly around the island's edge, stopping to view the **Hālona Blow Hole** (see p39) and watch the bodysurfers and kite-fliers at **Sandy Beach**.

At **Makapu'u Wayside**, park and make the easy hour-long, two-mile trek up and down the old lighthouse road; the views will stay with you long after you return home.

Afterward, stop for a drink or bite to eat at **Zippy's** (p101) and refresh yourself with a swim at one of the **Waimānalo** beach parks before heading home via the Pali Highway.

Left **Vue Hawaii** Right **Naturally Hawaiian Gallery & Gifts**

Places to Shop

Compleat Kitchen
Honolulu's first upscale kitchen supply store stocks gorgeous bamboo cutting boards and other high-quality gifts for foodies. ◎ *Kāhala Mall, 4211 Wai'alae Ave. • Map E6 • 737 5827*

Ohelo Road
Stylish women's clothing boutique, featuring very chic imports. ◎ *Kāhala Mall, 4211 Wai'alae Ave. • Map E6 • 735 5525*

Vue Hawaii
A careful selection of gifts with island themes, many of them hand-made in Hawai'i by local artisans. ◎ *Kāhala Mall, 4211 Wai'alae Ave. • Map E6 • 735 8774*

Paperie
A lovely shop, chock full of fine quality paper goods, Hawai'i-themed cards, stationery, and wedding supplies. ◎ *Kāhala Mall, 4211 Wai'alae Ave. • Map E6 • 735 6464*

Hawai'i Kai Towne Center and Hawai'i Kai Shopping Center
These side-by-side open malls offer grocery shopping, dive shops, boat charter firms, and restaurants, as well as banking and dry cleaning services. ◎ *Towne Center: 6700 Kalaniana'ole Hwy; Shopping Center: 377 Keahole • Map F5 • 396 0766*

Koko Marina Center
Another shopping center, with a vast supermarket, theater complex, many eateries, and places to rent water gear or arrange excursions along the coast. ◎ *7192 Kalaniana'ole Hwy • Map F6 • 395 4737*

Mel's Market
For a taste of old-fashioned island grocery stores, visit Mel's Market, a friendly one-stop store that offers hard-to-find ingredients for authentic *lū'au* dishes (salt meat and fish, raw crab, *kukui* nut relish, dried fish, and fish cake). ◎ *41-1029 Kalaniana'ole Hwy, Waimānalo • Map F5 • 259 7550*

Naturally Hawaiian Gallery & Gifts
This exceptional shop offers one-of-a-kind keepsakes, original artwork, books, and jewelry. It's also the place for Waimānalo rodeo posters and Hawaiian T-shirts. ◎ *41-1025 Kalaniana'ole Hwy, Waimānalo • Map F5 • 259 5354*

Sumo Connection
This shop is a shrine to the career of a Samoan from Hawai'i who found fame in Japan as sumo wrestler Yokozuna Akebono. Sumo souvenirs and island bric-a-brac are sold. ◎ *41-1537 Kalaniana'ole Hwy, Waimānalo • Map F5 • 259 8646*

Roadside Stands
Watch for charming roadside stands near Waimānalo. They sell fresh *kahuku* corn, fruits, chilled coconuts, tropical flowers, fresh or dried fish, and such ethnic specialties as *pasteles* (Puerto Rican tamales) and *poke* (raw fish and seaweed salad). ◎ *Map F5*

Price Categories

Price categories include a three-course meal for one, a glass of house wine, and all unavoidable extra charges including tax.

$	under $20
$$	$20–$30
$$$	$30–$45
$$$$	$45–$60
$$$$$	over $60

3660 on the Rise

TOP 10 Places to Eat

1 3660 on the Rise
Tucked away on the bottom floor of an office building in homey Kaimukī, this always-busy bistro pleases locals and visitors with smart variations on beloved local themes – sashimi *katsu*-style, chocolate-filled won tons, steak in Hawaiian salt. ◈ *3660 Wai'alae Ave. • Map E6 • 737 1177 • Closed Mon • $$$$*

2 The Counter
You can build your own burger here, or try one of their signature offerings: the Loco Moco combines a ground beef patty, fried egg, onion strings, and gravy on a bed of rice. ◈ *Kāhala Mall, 4211 Wai'alae Avenue • Map E6 • 739 5100 • $$*

3 Olive Tree Café
One of the few Mediterranean restaurants in the islands, this spot routinely wins awards for its great Greek fare and casual style. ◈ *4614 Kīlauea Ave., Kaimuki • Map E6 • 737 0303 • $$*

4 Hoku's
This sophisticated lunch and dinner restaurant ranks high among critics and diners for its world flavors, ocean view, and gracious service. ◈ *Kāhala Hotel & Resort, 5000 Kāhala Avenue • Map E6 • 739 8780 • $$$$$*

5 Plumeria Beach House
This oceanfront, indoor/outdoor restaurant is family-friendly and well known for lavish buffets. ◈ *Kāhala Hotel & Resort, 5000 Kāhala Ave. • Map E6 • 739 8760 • $$$*

6 Roy's Restaurant
The flagship of the sprawling Roy's Restaurant empire continues to deliver its trademarks: high-energy atmosphere, a dramatic open-plan kitchen, and a menu that ranges from salsa to Szechuan. ◈ *6600 Kalaniana'ole Highway, Hawai'i Kai • Map F5 • 396 7697 • $$$$*

7 Jack's Restaurant
Stop by this compact neighborhood spot to discover Jack's giant Special Biscuits, breakfast until 2pm, and freshly made local plates. ◈ *'Aina Haina Shopping Center, 820 W. Hind • Map E5 • 373 4034 • $*

8 Cha-Cha-Cha Salsaria
This light-hearted south of the border eatery offers inexpensive Mexican standards and fiery, fresh salsas – lots of them. ◈ *Hawai'i Kai Shopping Center, 377 Keahole St. • Map F5 • 395 7797 • $*

9 Kona Brewing Co.
The first O'ahu brewpub by Big Island-based Kona Brewing, located on one of Hawai'i Kai's man-made canals, serves burgers, salads, casual fare, and, of course, beer! ◈ *Koko Marina Center, 7192 Kalaniana'ole Hwy • Map F6 • 394 5662 • $$*

10 Zippy's
This seaside outpost of one of the island's most popular chains serves inexpensive, island-style comfort food (hamburger curry, won ton noodle soup) and house signature chili. ◈ *4134 Wai'alae Ave., Kāhala • Map E6 • 733 3730 • $*

Note: *Unless otherwise stated, all restaurants accept credit cards and serve vegetarian meals*

STREETSMART

STREETSMART

Left **Casual clothing** Right **Passenger aircraft**

TOP 10 Planning Your Visit

When to Visit
In terms of weather, Hawai'i is good to visit year round. May, June, September, and October are traditionally a bit slower than the height of winter and summer seasons, so better travel deals are often available.

Passport and Visa Requirements for Foreign Visitors
Visitors from the U.K., most Western European countries, Australia, New Zealand, Japan, and South Korea need a valid passport and must also register online with ESTA (https://esta.cbp.dhs.gov) in advance of travel to Hawai'i. Canadians must show a valid passport. Other foreign nationals need a valid passport and a tourist visa, obtainable from a U.S. consulate or embassy.

Customs/Agricultural Inspection
Foreign visitors may not bring food or plants of any kind into Hawai'i and luggage or cargo leaving the islands is subject to an agricultural search. Only certain fruits and flowers may be taken out, so ask about this when purchasing such items.

Climate
Contrary to popular belief, Hawai'i does have seasons. Rain is common Oct–Jan, and summer is much warmer than winter. Big surf arrives on north shores in winter; south swells delight surfers in summer. At sea level, temperatures average high 70s/low 80s in the daytime most of the year; nighttime temperatures can go down to the 60s, occasionally the 50s in winter.

Electricity
Standard U.S. current is 110–120 volts. Non-U.S. appliances need a converter and plug adapter with two flat pins, but bear in mind many hotels provide coffee makers, irons, and hair dryers.

Clothing
Hawai'i is a relaxed place. Shorts, T-shirts, swimsuits, and casual evening wear are all that's needed. Only a handful of restaurants require men to wear jackets. A sweater or jacket is a good idea for cool evenings.

Insurance
The cost of medical care is high everywhere in the U.S., including Hawai'i. Travel insurance is highly recommended. If you have a mainland health insurance plan, you should check to see if it's accepted in Hawai'i.

Major Airlines
The airline industry is facing difficult times and flight schedules and routes change frequently. At the time of writing, all major U.S. airlines, most Asian and Pacific lines, and some European carriers fly directly into Honolulu International Airport.

Enhanced Security
Although Hawai'i is a safe place, in the aftermath of 9/11, airport security has been enhanced, and items like pocket-knives, scissors, nail files, and tweezers must be packed in checked luggage. Those arriving on a visa may also have their photograph and fingerprints taken. When traveling inter-island, you should get to the airport one hour before your scheduled flight.

Cruise Lines
Crystal Cruises, Princess Cruises, and Royal Caribbean have ships that stop in Hawai'i as part of wider itineraries. Norwegian Cruise Lines operates vessels through the Hawaiian islands.

Directory

United Airlines
www.ual.com

American Airlines
www.aa.com

Delta Airlines
www.delta.com

Crystal Cruises
www.crystalcruises.com

Princess Cruises
www.princess.com

Royal Caribbean
www.royalcaribbean.com

Norwegian Cruise Lines
www.ncl.com

Left **Local magazines** Right **Friendly waitresses**

🔟 Sources of Information

1 Visitors Bureaus
The Hawai'i Visitors and Conventions Bureau (HVCB) is the "mother" of all the individual island bureaus. The HVCB serves as the official source of information for individual travelers, groups and conventioneers. The O'ahu Visitors Bureau is the island's chapter of HVCB.

2 Magazines
Hana Hou!, Hawaiian Airlines in-flight magazine is published six times a year. *HONOLULU* is Hawai'i's only major regional magazine and a great source of insider information. All can be accessed online.

3 Newspapers
Hawai'i has one main daily, the *Honolulu Star-Advertiser*, which has a morning and afternoon version and is available statewide. There are also several more locally oriented papers, most notably the "alternative" *Honolulu Weekly*, *MidWeek*, and the *Downtown Planet*.

4 Websites
Virtually all hotel chains, activities sellers, and even most restaurants now have their own websites. They are easily accessed via any search engine. The O'ahu Visitors Bureau site also offers links to many visitor attractions.

5 Suggested Reading
James Michener's *Hawai'i* is considered by many a "must-read" for visitors. It is certainly epic in scope and an entertaining, if not precisely accurate, historical novel. *Shoal of Time* by Gavan Daws, *Hawai'i's History by Hawai'i's Queen* by Queen Liliu'okalani, and *Hawaiian Mythology* by Martha Beckwith are all excellent choices.

6 Free Visitor Publications
You will be deluged by dozens of free visitor publications as soon as you arrive at any airport in Hawai'i. Many are chock full of discount coupons and free offers. Bear in mind that most publications cover only the places that advertise with them.

7 Concierge
Your hotel concierge is potentially one of the very best sources of insider information. They are, of course, island residents, and many know every nook and cranny of O'ahu – where to get the best noodles and find that vintage piece of Hawaiiana you're after. Remember to tip them woll if the advice is good.

8 Talk to Locals
Hawai'i is known for having some of the world's friendliest locals, and most love to share their knowledge of their hometown. Talk to waiters and waitresses, the bartender, the supermarket cashier, and the person who sells you your very first *aloha* shirt. You're sure to learn secrets not available in any guidebook!

9 Local TV
Oceanic Cable TV Channel 16 is a treasure trove of entertaining local information. Check it out, even if the pidgin (the local slang) proves a little difficult to decipher.

10 Yellow Pages
There's a Yellow Pages phone book in most hotel rooms. Besides helping to identify the closest Japanese restaurant or surf shop, flipping through the book will give you an idea of the local way of life. Keep in mind that the large display listings are paid advertising.

Directory

HVCB Visitors Bureau
- *1-800-GOHAWAII*
- *923 1811*
- *www.gohawaii.com*

O'ahu Visitors Bureau
- *1-877-525-6248*
- *524 0722*
- *www.visit-oahu.com*

Magazine and Newspaper Websites
- *www.hanahou.com*
- *www.spiritofaloha.com*
- *www.honolulu magazine.com*
- *www.staradvertiser. com*
- *www.honolulu weekly.com*

Left **Airplanes at Honolulu International Airport** Right **Cruise ship, Honolulu**

⒑ Arriving in O'ahu

Domestic Airlines
All major U.S. airlines as well as Hawai'i's own Hawaiian and go! Mokulele fly directly into Honolulu International Airport from many U.S. cities. Several North American charter companies also bring visitors to O'ahu daily.

Foreign Airlines
Many foreign carriers – most notably the Pacific and Asian companies like Qantas, Air New Zealand, Air Pacific, Japan Airlines, China Airlines, Korean Air, and Philippine Airlines – land at Honolulu International Airport. Air Canada, Lufthansa, Sabena, and Swissair are some others offering flights into Honolulu.

Inter-Island Airlines
Hawaiian Airlines, Island Air, and go! Mokulele fly between all the major islands from early morning until evening every day. Schedules change often; weekend, non-stop, and first and last flights of the day fill up quickly.

Information at the Airport
Information booths can be found in the baggage claim areas, outside the foreign arrivals area, in the Inter-island Terminal, near Gate 22, and at both ends of the airport's main lobby. There are also many racks of free visitor publications.

Airport Shuttles
The WikiWiki Shuttle buses (*wikiwiki* means "quick") connect the terminals at the airport. Airport Island Shuttles take you from the airport to all parts of O'ahu.

Cruise Ships
Crystal Cruises, Carnival Cruises, Celebrity Cruises, Regent, Princess, and Royal Caribbean include Honolulu on some of their cruises. Norwegian Cruise Lines offers weekly cruises around Hawai'i.

Maps
Free maps come in virtually every drive guide for rental vehicles and in visitor publications. For more detailed maps, look in bookstores such as Barnes & Noble, or ask for a photocopy of the one in the front of the phone book.

Directions
Folks in Hawai'i don't give directions in terms of east, west, north, south. Instead, you will hear the words "*'ewa*" (toward 'Ewa), "diamond head" (toward Diamond Head), "*mauka*" (toward the mountains), and "*makai*" (toward the ocean).

Greeters
Contrary to what you may see in old movies, *lei* greeters do not welcome every new arrival. If, however, you are on a package tour, you will likely be greeted with a *lei* and a peck on the cheek from a company employee. And if you're visiting friends or family, you will surely receive a garland upon arrival.

Passports/Visas
Visitors from the U.K, most Western European countries, Australia, New Zealand, Japan, and South Korea need a valid passport and must also register with ESTA (see p104). Canadians are required to show a valid passport. Other foreign nationals need a valid passport and tourist visa.

Directory

Inter-Island Airlines
• *Island Air, 484 2222, 1 800 652 6541, www.islandair.com*
• *go! Mokulele, 888 435 9462, www.iflygo.com*
• *Hawaiian Airlines, 800 882 8811, www.hawaiianair.com*

Domestic Airlines
• *American, 1 800 223 5436, www.aa.com*
• *Delta, 1 800 325 1999, www.delta.com*
• *Northwest/KLM, 1 800 225 2525, www.nwa.com*
• *United, 1 800 241 6522, www.ual.com*

Airport Island Shuttle
• *834 8844*

Left **TheBus** Center **Pleasure Ship** Right **Sign pointing toward a public beach**

📋 Getting Around O'ahu

1 Rental Cars

Virtually every major national rental car company is represented in Honolulu. Local companies are less expensive but may be less reliable.

2 Trolleys

The cute open-air trolleys you'll spot rolling around Honolulu have been carrying visitors since the mid-1980s. Today, the Waikīkī Trolley covers attractions with something for everyone, from the city's historical sites to shopping centers all over the island. The three main routes cover the historic sites (red line), scenic attractions (green line), and shopping destinations (pink line). Other trolleys include one specially for visitors interested in duty-free shopping, and a guided tour of Waikele. It is also possible to charter a trolley.

3 TheBus

You can get just about anywhere on O'ahu by TheBus. You can purchase one-way tickets or a visitor's pass. The pass lets you ride all you want on any four consecutive days and is sold at all ABC Stores in Waikīkī and the one at Ala Moana Shopping Center. Convenience stores in Honolulu stock the bus map, which also has a handy guide to Honolulu attractions.

4 Shuttles and Taxis

For short, in-town trips you can always get a taxi in front of any major hotel, and restaurants are happy to call a taxi for you after your meal. Many hotels also provide shuttle service – usually to shopping destinations, sometimes to sights.

5 Motorcycles and Mopeds

Not for the faint of heart, motorcycles are a fun way to tour the island; mopeds do well on city streets. Be aware: motorcycle rentals are much more expensive than a car or even a van.

6 Rules of the Road

Seatbelts for everyone and approved car seats for children under three are mandatory. Pedestrians always have the right of way. Right turns are permitted – unless otherwise noted – after a full stop at a stop sign or red light.

7 Refueling

It's a good idea to keep your car's gas tank at least half full as distances between gas stations may be long.

8 Local Etiquette on the Road

Like any big city, Honolulu has its traffic challenges, especially when work-day commuters come in and go out of town. Outside the metropolis, local people are rarely in a hurry, so allow plenty of time for any driving trip. Residents will never sound their car horns except in a case of imminent danger; thus you should check your rear-view mirror often to see if someone wants to pass you.

9 Guided Tours

By land, by sea, by air, even under the sea – every variety of guided tour is available on O'ahu (see pp42 & 114). There are even tours that specialize in shopping! You can do some advance research on the internet (try www.top-10-hawaii.com as a starting point). You'll also be inundated with information about tours at the airport.

10 Beach Access

All Hawaiian beaches are public. The problem, sometimes, is not being able to get to them without trespassing. Look out for public beach access signs, which are prominently displayed, and follow the paths.

Directory

Trolleys
• 591 2561 • www.waikikitrolley.com

TheBus
• 848 5555
• www.thebus.org

Many place names and some common words are Hawaiian, though few people speak fluent Hawaiian. See glossary p128.

Left **Cash point** Center **Post box** Right **Newspapers**

Banking & Communications

1 Banks
Bank of Hawai'i and First Hawaiian Bank are Hawai'i's largest, with branches throughout the islands, some of them inside supermarkets. In general, all banks are open: Mon–Thu 8:30am–3pm or 4pm, Fri 8:30am–6pm. Some branches have Saturday hours.

2 Credit Cards
VISA and MasterCard are accepted almost universally except by the smallest stores and roadside stands. American Express, Discover, Diner's Club, and JCB (a Japanese card) are accepted at most places but check first.

3 Travelers' Checks
By far the safest form of money, travelers' checks in U.S. currency are accepted virtually everywhere. Change is given in cash. Lost or stolen travelers' checks are easily replaced.

4 Telephone Calls
With the extraordinary proliferation of cell phones, public phones are fast disappearing. If you can find one, a local call will cost 50 cents, much cheaper than using a hotel phone. Inter-island calls are deemed long distance, and numbers must be preceded by dialing 1 808.

5 Postal Services
Posting a letter costs the same as on the mainland, but mail sometimes takes longer to reach its destination. Hotels will often post mail for you, but otherwise there are post offices in every town. Opening hours are generally: 8:30am–4:30pm Mon–Fri, with short morning hours at some branches on Saturdays.

6 Newspapers and Magazines
The best place to buy mainland newspapers and a wide array of magazines is at one of the numerous ABC stores that dot the island, or at Barnes & Noble (Kāhala Mall). The *Honolulu Star-Advertiser* (published twice a day) is the state's largest daily. For more on newspapers and magazines, *see p105.*

7 Television and Radio
In addition to the myriad U.S. television stations on the dial, Oceanic Cable Channel 16 provides the most local programming imaginable. All the major hotels have their own closed-circuit visitor channels with programming that provides an overview of the island, activities, shopping, and restaurants. Fans of every music genre, from rock to country to Hawaiian, will find something on the radio dial to satisfy them. If you want to listen like the locals do, try KINE, 101.5 FM for the best in island sounds.

8 "Coconut Wireless"
This is Hawai'i's version of "hearing it through the grapevine." Talk to as many locals as you can; you'll be pleasantly surprised at how willing most are to share the island's secrets.

9 Internet Access
Most hotel rooms and condos are wired for dial-up Internet access. Most large hotels have business centers where you can stay in touch with the office. Internet service is also available at several cafés.

10 Hawai'i Time
Unlike the U.S. mainland, Hawai'i does not subscribe to Daylight Savings Time – island time remains constant throughout the year. From October to April, Hawai'i is two hours behind the U.S. West Coast (10 behind G.M.T); from April to October three hours (11 G.M.T).

Directory

Banks
• Bank of Hawai'i
808 643 3888
• First Hawaiian Bank
808 844 4444

Lost Cards & Checks
• American Express
800 528 4800 (cards)
800 221 7282
(travelers' checks)
• VISA, 800 336 8472
• MasterCard
800 826 2181

Left **Sign at private land** Center **Beach warning signs** Right **Well-prepared hikers**

TOP 10 Things to Avoid

1 Sunburn
Everyone is at risk of sunburn in the tropics. It's important to apply sunscreen often, including after swimming. A hat and sunglasses are good accessories, too. If you're especially fair, you should wear light, long-sleeved shirts and long pants when you're in the sun. Parents should be particularly careful with young children. Be vigilant on cloudy days, too – those ultraviolet rays get through the clouds.

2 Flash Floods
During heavy rains, Hawai'i's rivers are occasionally susceptible to flash floods. It's best not to venture out on hikes or unfamiliar drives during heavy rains. Hawai'i radio and television stations always announce flash flood watches and warnings; you can also check recorded national weather forecasts by calling 973 5286.

3 Heat Stroke
Although Hawai'i is blessed with cooling trade winds most days of the year, temperatures can easily reach into the 90s, especially in summer. It's always advisable to stay out of the sun from 11am until 2pm when, obviously, the sun is at its highest point over the islands. Wearing light-colored clothing and drinking lots of water are also recommended.

4 Dehydration
With heat and sun comes the possibility of dehydration. Always carry water with you, whether you're going for a drive, venturing out on a hike, or just relaxing at the beach. Drink often and drink plenty.

5 Bites and Stings
Scorpions and centipedes are Hawai'i's most troublesome insect pests. It is unlikely that you will run into either but, if you do get stung, get medical attention as quickly as possible. Mosquitoes are more bothersome than dangerous, and can be controlled with commercial repellants.

6 Trespassing
It's not difficult to accidentally wander onto private property, especially when hiking or going to the beach. Watch for No Trespassing signs, and always use the proper public beach accesses. You may see the word *Kapu* on signs, which is loosely translated as "forbidden."

7 Littering
The physical beauty of the islands is most certainly one of the main reasons visitors are so drawn to them. Nothing is more jarring to that beauty than litter strewn along beaches, hiking paths, and streets. There's no shortage of litter bins for food wrappers, cigarette stubs etc., so make use of them. (*Mahalo*, often printed on the bins, means thank you.)

8 Removing Natural Objects
Traditional Hawaiians believe that everything – every stone, every shell, every plant – has both a life and a place of its own. So feel free to look, enjoy, and touch natural objects, but refrain from removing anything from its home.

9 Jellyfish
Hawaiian waters are susceptible to invasions of jellyfish – both box jellyfish and Portuguese man-of-war – usually about a week after a full moon. Local radio and television stations are very reliable in reporting these incursions. Jellyfish stings can be painful and, if one is allergic, quite dangerous. The best way to treat them is with meat tenderizer (available at any supermarket) or, indeed, urine.

10 Sharp Coral
The islands are surrounded by reefs of coral, much of it very sharp. It can cause nasty cuts that are susceptible to infection, as coral is a living organism. Clean out a coral cut quickly and completely, treat it with an antiseptic, and keep it covered up. If a coral cut does get infected, it should be treated by a medical practitioner.

Left **Market entrance** Right **Cheap Chinese eats**

TOP 10 Shopping & Dining Tips

1 Opening Times
Large shopping centers are open, in general, Mon–Sat 9am–9pm; Sunday hours are usually shorter. Some supermarkets and convenience stores stay open 24 hours. Most retail stores are open on U.S. holidays (with the possible exception of Christmas Day and New Year's Day) and Hawai'i state holidays, such as Prince Kūhiō Day (Mar 26) and King Kamehameha Day (Jun 11).

2 Alcohol and Smoking Laws
The legal drinking age in Hawai'i is 21. The age limit applies, as well, to buying alcoholic drinks – including beer and wine – at retail outlets. Smoking is prohibited in all O'ahu restaurants, including bars and outdoor dining areas.

3 Early Bird Specials
Not surprisingly, everyone wants to dine at sunset. In order to encourage pre-sunset dinner reservations, many restaurants offer "early bird" specials *(see entry 3 opposite)*.

4 Sales Tax
There's general excise tax – 4 percent statewide and 4.5 percent in O'ahu at the time of writing – on everything, without exception, in Hawai'i. That includes food – be it a restaurant meal or groceries from the market – all retail goods (even medicine), and all services.

5 Evening Dining Hours
"Early to bed, early to rise" is the credo throughout the Aloha State. Don't be surprised if the restaurant on which you have your romantic heart set for a late night dinner stops serving at 8:30 or 9pm. The same is true of breakfast and lunch – many local folks take their lunch break at 11 or even 10:30am.

6 Casual and Formal Dining
There are few restaurants on O'ahu that require anything fancier than a shirt with a collar and footwear of some kind; there are only a handful that would frown on shorts and sandals.

7 Tipping
Those who work in the visitor industry – everyone from the hardworking hotel housekeepers to the handsome young men who park cars – depend on tips to supplement their wages, so generosity is greatly appreciated. Restaurant tips should be at least 15 percent of the total bill. Parking valets should be tipped $1–$2; luggage handlers at least $2 per bag. And if you avail yourself of the service, you should tip your hotel concierge.

8 Shop at the Local Stores
You'll save money on souvenirs, resort wear, even groceries if you shop where the locals do. Local favorite Longs Drugs has locations all over O'ahu and is a great source for macadamia nuts, coffee, and lots more. There are farmers' markets dotted around the island, and there's a big weekend swap meet at Aloha Stadium for excellent buys on flowers, local produce, and crafts.

9 Cheap Eats
Hawai'i's ethnic restaurants serve delicious food at low prices. You'll find Vietnamese, Chinese, Japanese, Mexican, and local-style food all over O'ahu – best bets are Chinatown and Honolulu's suburbs. At more expensive restaurants, ordering several appetizers and sharing them is an inexpensive way to sample dishes.

10 Check When Buying Souvenirs
Unfortunately, much of what passes for Made in Hawai'i goods is actually manufactured in China, Taiwan, or the Philippines. A "Made-in-Hawai'i" label may, indeed, be fake. Always ask to be sure you're getting the genuine article, and stick to places like museum gift shops and local art and craft galleries.

Left **Coupons** Right **Market stalls**

🔟 Budget Tips

1 Rent a Condo
Condominiums tend to be less expensive than hotel rooms. Rentals are readily available on O'ahu – get out of Honolulu and the expensive areas of Diamond Head, Koko Head, Kahala, Hawai'i Kai and Kailua for the best deals. Condos range from studios to three bedroom apartments. They're almost universally well maintained and equipped.

2 Eat In
The cost of dining out can easily rack up, so eating in is the obvious alternative, especially if you're renting a condo. Throughout O'ahu, there are lots of supermarkets, grocery stores, and farmers' markets where the fixings for a great meal can be easily found.

3 Ask about Discounts
Hotels, restaurants, and activity desks often offer discounts, especially during the slower months (May, June, September, October). Restaurants routinely offer "early bird" specials for folks who like to dine before the prime 6:30–8pm slot. Late night specials are common, but less well advertised.

4 Plan Well Before You Travel
Virtually every airline, many hotels, and even some car rental companies offer better prices to travelers who book well in advance.

It's also a good idea to check out restaurants and activities – many have websites – before arriving to avoid price surprises. Some advance research also allows you to comparison shop for things like whale watching and other costly activities.

5 Use Visitor Coupons
When you arrive at any airport in Hawai'i, you will see racks and racks of free visitor publications. Every one of them has coupons for discounts on restaurant meals and activities. If you have the time and the inclination to peruse the pages, the savings can be substantial.

6 Frequent Flyer and Corporate Discounts
Frequent flyer miles can be used for both free or upgraded air travel on all the major U.S. airlines. If you are a member of a national organization such as AARP (for the over 50s) or work for a large corporation, ask about discounts. You may find that your company ID card can save you money!

7 Book a Package Tour
Package tours are always less expensive than purchasing air and ground transportation and accommodations separately; any good travel agent will have lots to choose from. But even if you do choose

to book your own trip, inter-island package tours (from local companies like Pleasant Island Holidays and Roberts Hawai'i) are a great and affordable way to experience another island.

8 Shop the Internet
The internet has become a fantastic resource for excellent travel deals. The big, discount travel sites (Orbitz, Expedia, Hotels.com) always have discounted prices on air fares and hotel rooms. Many of the major airlines also offer special internet fares.

9 Travel Off-Season
Hawai'i is most expensive during the winter months when travelers from cold climes swoop down upon these sun-drenched, tropical islands. The summer months (July and August) are family travel time, since children are out of school. This leaves May, June, September, and October for the bargain hunters.

10 Book a Non-Ocean View Room
Oceanfront rooms are the most expensive accommodations in Hawai'i. Next come ocean view rooms and then partial ocean view rooms. In high-rise hotels, the upper floors are also priced at a premium. Booking a mountain or garden room view could save you hundreds of dollars on your bill.

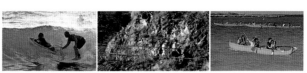

Left **Surfing** Center **Hiking** Right **Canoeing**

TOP 10 Outdoor Activities

1 Cruises/Sailing
From small, close-to-the-ocean-action Zodiacs to Navatek's 140-foot SWATH (Small Water-plane Area Twin Hull), every manner of sailing and cruising adventure is available in Hawai'i. Excursions depart from all areas of the island; during the winter months most cruises combine whale-watching with other activities.

2 Hiking
With more than 30 major trails covering terrain of every description, it's no wonder that hiking is as popular an activity with locals as it is with visitors. You can get a free map that will point you to all of O'ahu's most popular hikes from the State Department of Land and Natural Resources (587 0166, www.hawaii.gov/dlnr).

3 Surfing/Windsurfing
Whether you've always wanted to learn to surf or you're already an expert, many feel there's no better place on Earth to catch a wave than the Island of O'ahu. From the gentle rolling waves at Waikīkī to the monster winter sets of Waimea Bay, instruction at your level is available. There are plenty of places to rent equipment, too. For windsurfing, head to – where else? – the Windward side.

4 Snorkeling
Hawai'i's most famous snorkeling spot – Hanauma Bay – is also the most popular. While this is perfect for beginners, more experienced snorkelers probably won't enjoy the crowds. There are other good snorkeling locations around the island, most notably Maunalua Bay, east of Diamond Head.

5 Scuba
In addition to a myriad variety of reef fish and other sea creatures, O'ahu is a great location for divers to explore shipwrecks. One of the most notable wrecks is the 150+-foot Mahi which was purposely sunk in 1982 off the leeward side (south of Wai'anae) to create an artificial reef. While the diving off the North Shore is good, it is best left to experienced divers and only in summer months, at that.

6 Air Tours
Sailplanes, seaplanes, and helicopters offer aerial tours of O'ahu. Any of these will provide you with an excellent panorama of the island from a unique perspective and a chance to observe inaccessible natural areas.

7 Fishing
Fishing is good year round in the waters surrounding O'ahu as well as all the neighboring islands. Sportfishing charters can be quite costly but can provide the thrill of a lifetime for anglers who've never had a deep-sea fishing experience before. Half- and full-day charters are available.

8 Walking Tours
Chinatown and downtown are good places to discover on foot. Other walking tours focus on Honolulu's historical and cultural sites, or the city's unique architecture. The National Geographic Society offers a walking tour of historic temples and archaeological sites.

9 Tennis
More than 180 public courts on the island cater to tennis enthusiasts. You can get a free listing of all of them from the City and County of Honolulu Department of Parks and Recreation (768 3003). The larger resort hotels have tennis courts for use by their guests; some welcome non-guests for a fee.

10 Bicycling
Honolulu is a major metropolitan area and unless you enjoy dodging traffic, city bicycling may not be the best idea. Mountain bikes can be rented for excursions outside the city and North Shore guided bike tours are available, too.

For more advice on water sports and other outdoor activities **see pp40–53**

Left **Big waves sign** Center **Snorkeling buddies** Right **Sunbathers**

🔟 Safety Tips

1 Ocean Safety
With care and common sense, it's easy to enjoy the Pacific waters, but remember that strong currents, big waves, undertow, sharp coral, and potentially dangerous sea creatures are all natural parts of Hawai'i's environment. Also, many beaches are not staffed by lifeguards. A red flag on the beach indicates strong currents, and posted signs will alert you to other dangers.

2 Medical Emergencies
As in the rest of the U.S., dialing 911 in Hawai'i will put you in touch with the emergency services. There are several major medical centers in Honolulu – Queen's, Kapi'olani, and St. Francis, to name a few. There are clinics all over the island too, and resort hotels mostly have doctors on call.

3 Climate and Quakes
Blessed with a near perfect climate all year round, Hawai'i is, however, susceptible to extreme weather and natural disasters, most notably hurricanes (from June to November), tidal waves, and earthquakes (usually benign). O'ahu's Upcountry districts are cool throughout the year and can be very cold at the higher elevations, especially in the winter.

4 Smart Hiking
Good shoes are recommended, especially for serious hikers; rain forest trails can get very muddy and slick. Carry plenty of water and snacks and be absolutely sure of your route before you begin. Never hike alone and make sure someone knows where you're going and what time you're expected back.

5 Sun Sense
The sun in the tropics is stronger than anywhere else, even when it doesn't feel that way and even when the sky is overcast. Using sunscreen is an absolute must, as is re-application throughout the day. Fair-skinned people should wear a hat and light-colored, long-sleeved clothing where possible. And remember to drink water throughout the day.

6 Theft and Valuables
Unfortunately, even in Paradise, theft is a problem and tourists' rental cars are often the targets. Always lock your car, even if leaving it for just a few moments. Never leave anything of value in view. A locked trunk may not be a deterrent so, if possible, take anything of value with you. Make use of your hotel's safes, or lock boxes in rental properties, to store cash, jewelry, traveler's checks, and other treasures.

7 Water
All hotels and most other accommodations have filtration systems so the tap water is perfectly safe unless otherwise indicated. Bottled water is handy for carrying with you on day trips. Never drink from streams, ponds, rivers, waterfalls, or freshwater pools.

8 Lock Your Doors
Hawai'i is a very casual and, in general, an extremely safe place. All the same, you should lock your hotel room or condo – that includes balcony doors, too.

9 Safe Neighborhoods
Crime is not nearly the problem it is in some other U.S. cities, but Honolulu IS a big city, and, as such, has its share of less salubrious neighborhoods. Check with your hotel concierge about neighborhoods to avoid, especially at night.

10 Snorkeling and Scuba Safety
The buddy system ensures that you never dive alone and that you share responsibility for your safety. Full scuba instruction is widely available, but even if you're already a certified diver, familiarize yourself with the underwater terrain before any excursion.

Left **Whale watching** Center **Polynesian Cultural Center** Right **Honolulu Harbor**

🔟 Specialist Tours

1 Polynesian Adventure Tours

This company offers circle island tours, city sightseeing, even outlet shopping tours. Small groups, especially, will enjoy the mini-vans and mini-coaches.

2 Roberts Hawai'i

Roberts has been around for a long time and is reliable for guided land tours, sightseeing cruises, lū'au, and dinner shows. Their "overnight-ers" are all-inclusive, economical overnight trips to neighboring islands.

3 E Noa Tours

This company, which tends to lead smaller groups, employs certified tour guides for their itineraries including a circle-the-island tour, Pearl Harbor, and the shopping outlets at Waikele. Mini-buses and trolleys are the modes of transport.

4 Native Hawaiian Hospitality Association

Visitors interested in the history and culture of the island can spend two glorious hours walking with the knowledgeable docents from NAHHA. There are two separate trails along the Waikīkī Heritage Trail, both free.

5 Aloha Bus

Hop-on/hop-off bus tours are offered in a variety of languages. The double-decker buses give visitors perfect views of Honolulu's top attractions, neighborhoods, and places of interest.

6 Honolulu Soaring Club

Soar above the island in a quiet sail plane and enjoy the views along the spectacular North Shore. Planes take off every 20 minutes from Dillingham Airfield in Mokulē'ia.

7 Island Seaplane Service

The planes take off and land on the water; tours are narrated, and include complimentary van transportation from your hotel.

8 Dolphin Excursions

You'll travel along the Leeward coast by Zodiac, a low-slung, motorized rubber boat that allows you to get up close to spinner dolphins and wintering whales. If conditions are right, you can even jump into the water with them! Book far in advance.

9 Honolulu Sailing Company

Luxury sail and power yachts are available by the hour, day or week. The company also offers group sail, snorkel and whale-watching tours.

10 Hawaiian Fire Surf School

You can learn to surf on a secluded beach with baby waves by instructors who also work as firefighters! What could be safer? Or more fun? Transportation from your hotel is provided.

Directory

Polynesian Adventure Tours
833 3000 • 1 800 622 3011 • www.polyad.com

Roberts Hawaii
539 9400 • 1 800 831 5541 • www.roberts hawaii.com

E Noa Tours
591 2561 • 1 800 824 8804 • www.enoa.com

NAHHA
628 6370
• www.nahha.com

Aloha Bus
457 4300
• www.alohabus.com

Honolulu Soaring Club
677 3404 • www. honolulusoaring.com

Island Seaplane
836 6273 • www.island seaplane.com

Dolphin Excursions
239 5579 • www. dolphinexcursions.com

Honolulu Sailing Company
239 3900
• www.honsail.com

Hawaiian Fire Surf School
737 3473 • www. hawaiianfire.com

 For Honolulu walking tours see p42

Left **Tram** Center **Family on the beach** Right **Camping**

🔟 Accommodations Tips

1 Traveling with Children

Hawai'i is a family-friendly place. Restaurants offer *keiki* (child) menus, and the resort hotels have *keiki* programs to keep the kids busy while the adults relax. In most hotels, small children can stay in their parents' room at no extra charge. Condos are a good, less expensive choice for families.

2 Visitors with Disabilities

Hawai'i extends a warm *aloha* to travelers with disabilities. Due in large part to the ADA (Americans with Disabilities Act), hotels, restaurants, and attractions provide wheelchair ramps, special parking places, and accessible restrooms. Braille translations of elevator button panels and other important signs are commonplace.

3 Hidden Extras

Accommodations are subject to a sales tax and room tax, so be prepared for an additional 13.75 percent on your bill. Most accommodations charge more than the standard rate for phone calls, faxes, and internet access. There may also be a daily parking charge.

4 Rates

At the low end of the spectrum are campsite permits, and at the high end are luxury resort suites, villas, and bungalows. Mid-price range hotel rooms are about $250 a night, while one-bedroom condos are about $200. Inns and B&Bs often have lovely rooms for $100 to $150 a night.

5 Travel Packages

Travel packages typically include air and ground transportation and accommodations; some even include inter-island travel, activities, and some meals. The price usually depends on the accommodations and size of rental vehicle.

6 Deciphering Local Descriptions

The description "ocean-front" means you will have a panoramic and unobstructed view of the blue Pacific. And you will, of course, pay a premium for it. Other descriptions include "ocean view" and "partial ocean view". You will not be able to see the ocean from a "garden" or "mountain view room." Some rooms have no view at all.

7 Discounts

Frequent flier programs, corporate identification cards, and fraternal organization memberships are just a few of the ways you can avail yourself of discounted room rates. The websites of chain hotels will often offer these kinds of deals, and so will many travel agents.

8 Reservation Services

Most of the resort hotels are part of famous chains, and reservations can easily be made online. Travel agents can book most accommodations available. Many hotels, condos, inns, and B&Bs have their own websites and accept reservations directly. The O'ahu Visitors Bureau can also help.

9 Tips & Taxes

Tipping hotel personnel is usual – averages are $2 to $3 a day for housekeepers, $1 to $2 for parking valets, $1 to $2 per piece of luggage for baggage handlers, and 15 percent for room service servers. Most guests tip the concierge, as well, if they use their services. Everything in Hawai'i – all goods and services – is subject to 4 percent sales tax (4.5 percent in O'ahu). Hotels also charge a room tax of 9.25 percent.

10 Laundry & Dry Cleaning

All the resort hotels offer laundry and dry cleaning services, but these are usually very expensive. Most condominium complexes have coin-operated laundries on the property; it will cost a few dollars per load to wash and dry. There are also coin-operated laundromats scattered around the island.

Left **Royal Hawaiian Hotel** Right **Sheraton Moana Surfrider**

🔟 Luxury Resorts and Hotels

Halekulani
Located on the beach, the Halekulani defines elegance. It has manicured tropical grounds, tastefully simple decor, a spa, superb cuisine at La Mer (see p59), and its signature "orchid pool." ✆ 2199 Kālia Rd. • Map J7 • 923 2311 • www.halekulani.com • $$$$$

Hawai'i Prince Hotel Waikīkī
Every room at this marina-front hotel overlooks the picturesque Ala Wai Yacht Harbor. There are two award-winning restaurants: Prince Court offers Hawai'i cuisine, Hakone traditional Japanese. The hotel is right by the huge Ala Moana Shopping Center, Waikīkī nightlife, and downtown Honolulu. ✆ 100 Holomoana St. • Map G6 • 956 1111 • www.princeresortshawaii.com • $$$$

Sheraton Moana Surfrider
Here the rich Hawaiian details combine with every modern comfort. Teatime on the Banyan Veranda will carry you back in time; enjoying contemporary Hawaiian entertainment in the same stunning setting is a highlight of any visit. ✆ 2365 Kalākaua Ave. • Map K7 • 922 3111 • www.moana-surfrider.com • $$$$

Aulani Disney Resort & Spa
With over 800 rooms and villas, this massive resort brings some Disney magic to the leeward coast. There is a keen focus on native culture, with firepit storytelling and a collection of Hawaiian artifacts. ✆ 92-1185 Ali'inui Dr., Ko Olina • Map B5 • 714 520 7001 • http://resorts.disney.go.com/aulani-hawaii-resort • $$$$$

Royal Hawaiian Hotel
The beloved "Pink Palace of the Pacific" has been a Waikīkī landmark since it opened in 1927. The stucco exterior, the interior decor, and even the towels are pink here. Its Royal Beach Tower is slightly pricier; many would say the Historic Wing has more charm. ✆ 2259 Kalākaua Ave. • Map K7 • 923 7311 • www.royal-hawaiian.com • $$$$

Kahala Hotel & Resort
On a great swimming beach and close to plenty of golf, this resort is perhaps best known for its lagoon, where guests can mix with bottlenose dolphins through the Dolphin Encounters program. The award-winning Hoku's restaurant is also here. ✆ 5000 Kāhala Ave. • Map E6 • 739 8888 • www.kahalaresort.com • $$$$$

The Outrigger Reef on the Beach
Located right on the beach near Ft. DeRussy, this hotel's highlights are a swimming pool, nightly Hawaiian entertainment, and the oceanside Serenity Spa. It is also known for its Hawaiian wedding vow renewal ceremonies. ✆ 2169 Kālia Rd. • Map J7 • 923 3111 • www.outrigger.com • $$$

Hyatt Regency Waikīkī Resort & Spa
An elaborate atrium with cascading waterfall joins the two 40-story towers of this impressive resort in the center of Waikīkī. The Shor American Seafood Grill features open-air seating with ocean views and an extensive menu. ✆ 2424 Kalākaua Ave. • Map L7 • 923 1234 • www.hyatt.com • $$$

Aston Waikīkī Beach Tower
This all-suite, luxury ocean-front property has only four suites per floor. Each one- or two-bedroom suite has a luxury kitchen, plus washer and dryer. ✆ 2470 Kalākaua Ave. • Map M7 • 926 6400 • www.astonhotels.com • $$$$

Waikīkī Parc
Although it's not on the beach, it is the sister of the luxurious Halekulani across the street. The level of service is the same at a much lower price. Rooms are tastefully appointed, and the Nobu Waikīkī offers bountiful buffets. ✆ 2233 Helumoa Rd. • Map J7 • 921 7272 • www.waikikiparc.com • $$$

Note: Unless otherwise stated, all hotels accept credit cards, and have en-suite bathrooms and air conditioning

Streetsmart

Price Categories

For a standard, double room per night (with breakfast if included), taxes, and extra charges.

$	under $100
$$	$100–$200
$$$	$200–$300
$$$$	$300–$400
$$$$$	over $400

Left **Hilton Hawaiian Village** Right **Sheraton Waikīkī**

🔟 More Luxury Hotels

1 Hilton Hawaiian Village

Situated on the widest stretch of Waikīkī Beach, this huge hotel has six towers, five pools, over 90 shops, 20 lounges and restaurants, a spa, and tropical gardens. You need never leave the complex. ❧ 2005 Kālia Rd. • Map H7 • 949 4321 • www.hiltonhawaiian village.com • $$$

2 The Hotel at Turtle Bay Resort

Set on a wide stretch of oceanfront on the North Shore of O'ahu, this resort has guest rooms, beach cottages, and ocean villas. There are great walking and running trails and plenty of sports activities. The on-site Spa Luana offers a wide range of services. ❧ 57-091 Kamehameha Hwy, Kahuku • Map C1 • 293 6000 • www. turtlebayhotel.com • $$$$

3 Turtle Bay Condos

Good for families or small groups, this service handles vacation rentals of condominiums on the grounds of the Turtle Bay Resort Golf Course and beach cottages on the North Shore. ❧ 56-565 Kamehameha Hwy • Map C1 • 293 2800 • www.turtlebay condos.com • $$–$$$

4 The Estates at Turtle Bay

These condominiums – all individually owned – are great value, ranging from studios to three-bedroom deluxe units. All have full kitchens. ❧ 56-565 Kamehameha Hwy • Map C1 • 293 0600 • www. turtlebay-rentals.com • $$

5 JW Marriott 'Ihilani Resort & Spa

With its romantic sunset views and beautiful lagoons, this sprawling property is a popular wedding spot. The rooms are large, with marble baths and high-tech systems to control the interior environment. There's an 18-hole championship golf course and a huge spa. ❧ 92-1001 'Oani St. • Map B5 • 679 0079 • www. ihilani.com • $$$$

6 Renaissance 'Ilikai Waikīkī

The guest rooms here are spacious and situated in two towers with views of Ala Wai Yacht Harbor and the ocean. Sarento's Top of the "I" restaurant is a popular dining spot. ❧ 1777 Ala Moana Blvd. • Map G6 • 949 3811 • www.ilikaihotel.com • $$

7 The Lotus at Diamond Head

This small luxury hotel at the foot of Diamond Head has light, airy rooms with Balinese furnishings. The location is superb – close enough to Waikīkī to enjoy it when you want to and far enough away when you don't. It's home to the Diamond Head Grill with its hip, see-and-be-seen bar (currently closed for renovation). ❧ 2885 Kalākaua Ave. • Map E6 • 922 1700 • www. castleresorts.com • $$$

8 Sheraton Waikīkī

Sleek and modern, this 1,700-room hotel towers over the beach at Waikīkī – most of the rooms have spectacular ocean views. Don't miss the Edge of Waikīkī infinity pool bar and grill where, in the evening, you can enjoy Waikīkī's sparkling lights. ❧ 2255 Kalākaua Ave. • Map K7 • 922 4422 • www.sheraton-waikiki.com • $$$

9 Aston Waikīkī Sunset

Perfect for families, this high-rise condominium features one- and two-bedroom suites with fully equipped kitchens. It's an easy walk to the beach and to Honolulu Zoo. There's also a playground and a barbecue area. ❧ 229 Paoakalani Ave. • Map M7 • 922 0511 • www.aston hotels.com • $$$

10 The Waikīkī Edition

In addition to stylish rooms, guests at this trendy resort can enjoy a sunrise pool and a sunset beach (with sand imported from neighboring islands). Iron Chef Morimoto's namesake restaurant (see p74) is a worthy in-house dining destination. ❧ 1775 Ala Moana Blvd. • Map G6 • 943 5800 • www.editionhotels.com/ hotels/waikiki • $$$$

Left **Outrigger Waikīkī on the Beach** Right **Waikīkī Beach Marriott Resort**

TOP 10 Mid-Price Hotels

1 Pacific Beach Hotel
In the center of Waikīkī, this hotel has a 280,000-gallon aquarium a full three stories tall that provides the decorative inspiration for the property. Features include a tennis court, pool and whirlpool, salon and spa, and lobby shopping. ⊗ 2490 Kalākaua Ave. • Map L7 • 922 1233 • www.pacificbeachhotel. com • $$$

2 New Otani Kaimana Beach Hotel
Although the rooms at this boutique hotel are small, the fabulous location on Sans Souci Beach – across from Kapi'olani Park with easy access to Honolulu Zoo and the Waikīkī Shell – more than makes up for them. The beachside Hau Tree Lanai restaurant has the best poi waffles in town. ⊗ 2863 Kalākaua Ave. • Map M7 • 923 1555 • www. kaimana.com • $$$

3 Waikīkī Joy Hotel
This off-the-main-drag boutique hotel is a hidden treasure. One of the two towers has suites, the other regular rooms. All have whirlpool tubs and stereos. Complimentary continental breakfast. ⊗ 320 Lewers St. • Map K6 • 923 2300 • www.resort questhawaii.com • $$$

4 Ala Moana Hotel
Conveniently located between Waikīkī and Downtown, this all-purpose hotel has two restaurants and a nightclub. Guests also have access to the huge Ala Moana Shopping Center. ⊗ 410 Atkinson Dr. • Map G5 • 955 4811 • www. alamoanahotel.com • $$$

5 Sheraton Princess Ka'iulani
This comfortable hotel has all the advantages of a Sheraton without the oceanfront prices. It's home to the revue Creation – A Polynesian Journey, a Japanese restaurant, and an all-you-can-eat buffet restaurant. ⊗ 120 Ka'iulani Ave. • Map L6 • 922 5811 • www. princess-kaiulani.com • $$$

6 Holiday Inn Waikīkī Beachcomber
Across the street from Waikīkī Beach and a short walk from the Royal Hawaiian Shopping Center and International Marketplace, this hotel has a 400-seat buffet and hosts a Magic of Polynesia show. ⊗ 2300 Kalākaua Ave. • Map K6 • 922 4646 • $$

7 Outrigger Waikīkī on the Beach
This oceanfront hotel is the jewel in the crown of the Outrigger chain. The 500 guest rooms feature Polynesian decor. The hotel's main ballroom has been home to the glitzy Society of Seven show for a quarter century. The beachfront Duke's Waikīkī restaurant is wildly popular and often hosts great contemporary Hawaiian entertainers. ⊗ 2335 Kalākaua Ave. • Map K7 • 923 0711 • www.outrigger.com • $$$

8 Hilton Waikīkī Prince Kūhiō
Located in the heart of Waikīkī, a short walk to Kūhiō Beach, this tasteful hotel has a modern American restaurant, several bars, and a 10th-floor pool deck. ⊗ 2500 Kūhiō Ave. • Map M6 • 922 0811 • www.princekuhio hotel.com • $$$

9 Hotel Renew
This boutique hotel offers an eco-friendly, upscale option for visitors to Waikīkī. With only 72 guest rooms, Renew provides an intimate atmosphere in keeping with its spirit of wellness and tranquility. ⊗ 4129 Paoakalani Ave. • Map M7 • 687 7700 • www.hotel renew.com • $$

10 Waikīkī Beach Marriott Resort
Across from Kūhiō Beach, this hotel's Ali'iolani Tower offers very large guest rooms; many Paokalani Tower rooms have great views of Diamond Head. There are six restaurants, two pools, a full-service spa, a fitness center, and plenty of on-site shopping. ⊗ 2552 Kalākaua Ave. • Map M7 • 922 6611 • www.marriott waikiki.com • $$$

Note: Unless otherwise stated, all hotels accept credit cards, and have en-suite bathrooms and air conditioning

Price Categories

For a standard, double room per night (with breakfast if included), taxes, and extra charges.

$	under $100
$$	$100–$200
$$$	$200–$300
$$$$	$300–$400
$$$$$	over $400

Left 'Ohana Waikīkī East Right 'Ilima Hotel

TOP 10 More Mid-Price Hotels

1 Waikīkī Shore Condominium

The only oceanfront condo complex in Waikīkī, most of the one- and two-bed suites and studios feature breathtaking views, especially on the upper floors. All units have a kitchen and laundry facilities. ◉ 2161 Kālia Rd. • Map J7 • 952 4500 • www.castleresorts.com • $$$

2 Park Shore

Located across from Kapi'olani Park at the Diamond Head end of Waikīkī, just steps from the beach, the Park Shore offers a premium location without premium prices. The rooms are comfortable; there's a 24-hour family restaurant on site. ◉ 2586 Kalākaua Ave. • Map M7 • 923 0411 • www.parkshorewaikiki.com • $$

3 'Ohana Waikīkī East

'Ohana means family in Hawaiian and this is a good choice for family vacations. Standard hotel rooms and studios with kitchenettes are available here. The Nintendo games in each room will keep the kids busy when you're not off sightseeing. It's a short walk to the beach. ◉ 150 Ka'iulani Ave • Map L6 • 922 5353 • www.ohanahotels.com • $$

4 Best Western Coconut Waikīkī

A favorite of inter-island business travelers; most of the rooms here have kitchenettes. Complimentary continental breakfast is served each morning. The location across from the Ala Wai Canal makes this convenient for a scenic early morning walk or jog. ◉ 450 Lewers St. • Map K6 • 923 8828 • www.aquaresorts.com • $$

5 Diamond Head Beach Hotel

No frills here but many feel the serene oceanfront setting away from the crowds of Waikīkī makes up for the simplicity. At the base of Diamond Head, it's just a short walk to the dining and shopping scenes of Kalākaua Avenue and across the street from Kapi'olani Park. ◉ 2947 Kalākaua Ave. • Map E6 • 922 1928 • www.obrhi.com • $$$

6 Aqua Bamboo and Spa

A smallish hotel offering studios and suites with contemporary island decor; the upper floors of this high-rise have great views. There's a swimming pool, sun deck, and whirlpool, and a relaxing spa offering therapeutic local treatments, such as Lomi Lomi massages. The beach is a short walk away. ◉ 2425 Kūhiō Ave. • Map L6 • 922 7777 • www.aquaresorts.com • $$

7 Waikīkī Gateway Hotel

On the corner of two main streets at the north end of Waikīkī, this high-rise has a range of rooms featuring park, beach, and ocean views. ◉ 2070 Kalākaua Ave. • Map J5 • 955 3741 • www.waikikigateway.com • $$

8 'Ewa Hotel

Tucked between Kalākaua and Kūhiō avenues, the attractions here are an earlier check-in time than most – 2pm (it's 3pm elsewhere) – the kitchen facilities, which in many of the rooms are particularly good, and the low rates. It's as close to Kapi'olani Park as you can get. ◉ 2555 Cartwright Rd. • Map M7 • 922 1677 • www.ewahotel.com • $$

9 'Ilima Hotel

Many consider this condominium hotel the best value in Waikīkī. All the studios, one-, two-, and three-bedroom suites are spacious, with kitchens. Local calls are included in the low prices and there is free Internet access. There's even a pool, exercise room, and sauna. ◉ 445 Nohonani St. • Map K6 • 923 1877 • www.ilima.com • $$$

10 Queen Kap'iolani Hotel

Overlooking Kapi'olani Park and Diamond Head, this high rise provides basic, clean accommodations. With a pool and sun deck, the hotel is a short walk to Waikīkī. ◉ 150 Kapahulu Ave. • Map M7 • 922 1941 • www.queenkapiolani.com • $$

Left **Ke 'Ike Beach Bungalows** Center **Manoa Valley Inn** Right **Pat's Kailua Beach Properties**

TOP 10 Budget Accommodations

1 Waikīkī Sand Villa Hotel

A few blocks from the beach, this hotel has medium-size rooms and studio apartments, all with free Internet access. Daily complimentary breakfast is served by the pool. ✆ 2375 Ala Wai Blvd. • Map K6 • 922 4744 • www. waikikisandvilla.com • $$

2 Aqua Island Colony

One of the tallest buildings in Waikīkī, this no-frills hotel overlooks the Ala Wai Canal, along which walkers and joggers exercise daily. Even the regular rooms have refrigerators and coffee makers. ✆ 445 Seaside Ave. • Map K6 • 923 2345 • www.aqua resorts.com • $$

3 Aston Pacific Monarch

With kitchenettes and high-definition televisions in every room, as well as a handy location near Waikīkī Beach, these condo-style units provide an affordable option for visiting families. There is also a rooftop area that includes a pool and sauna. ✆ 2427 Kūhiō Ave. • Map K6 • 877 997 6667 • www.astonhotels.com • $$

4 Pagoda Hotel and Terrace

Popular with locals due to its proximity to the shopping at Ala Moana, the Pagoda offers a variety of rooms – standard, studios with kitchenettes, and suites. The floating restaurant and water gardens are notable. ✆ 1525 Rycroft St. • Map B6 • 941 6611 • www. pagodahotel.com • $$

5 Turtle Bay Condominiums

Self-contained one- and two-bedroom units all have full kitchens, making them perfect for families. They're on the golf courses within the Turtle Bay Resort, near famous surfing beaches and major North Shore attractions. ✆ Turtle Bay Resort, 56-565 Kamehameha Hwy, Kahuku, 96731 • Map C1 • 293 0600 • www.turtlebay-rentals.com • $$

6 Manoa Valley Inn

This Victorian-style inn, with seven rooms and a single cottage, is situated in the shadow of the University of Hawai'i, providing guests with a quiet retreat from Honolulu's lights and action. Built in 1912, it is listed on the National Register of Historic Places. ✆ 2001 Vancouver Dr. • Map C6 • 947 6019 • www. manoavalleyinn.com • $$

7 Ali'i Bluffs Windward Bed & Breakfast

On the windward shore of O'ahu, this European-style B&B is a short drive from O'ahu's best beaches. The wonderful hosts have filled their home with antiques and art. ✆ 46-251 'Iki'iki St., Kāne'ohe • Map E4 • 235 1124 • www.hawaii scene.com/aliibluffs/ • $

8 North Shore Vacation Homes

You'll feel like a local when you rent a Hawaiian-style beach house in a quiet North Shore neighborhood. The rentals have large *lanai* (balconies), spectacular sunset views, and all the comforts of home. ✆ 59-229C Ke Nui Rd., Hale'iwa • Map C1 • 637 3507 • www.teamreal estate.com • $$

9 Ke 'Ike Beach Bungalows

These modest yet clean, comfortable beach cottages occupy their own stretch of beach between the surfing beaches of Waimea Bay and Banzai Pipeline. Run by a local resident, they offer serene, family-style Hawai'i. ✆ 59-579 Ke 'Iki Rd, Hale'iwa • Map B1 • 638 8829 • www.keiki beach.com • $$

10 Pat's Kailua Beach Properties

Groups of friends or families who'd like to try living like a local on O'ahu's windward side would do well to contact Pat's. The O'Malleys have fully furnished homes and cottages in beautiful residential areas of Kailua and Lanikai. ✆ 204 S. Kalaheo Ave., Kailua • Map F4 • 261 1653 • www.patskailua.com • $$

Note: Unless otherwise stated, all hotels accept credit cards, and have en-suite bathrooms and air conditioning

Price Categories

For a standard, double room per night (with breakfast if included), taxes, and extra charges.	
$	under $100
$$	$100–$200
$$$	$200–$300
$$$$	$300–$400
$$$$$	over $400

Left **Paradise Bay Resort** Right **The Breakers Hotel**

🔟 Inns and B&Bs

1 Paradise Bay Resort

In a rural setting on a peninsula 30 minutes from Waikīkī, this B&B offers a full kitchenette and spacious *lanai* for each room. Guests can enjoy on-site activities such as kayaking and stand-up paddle boarding. ◎ 47-039 Lihikai Dr., Kāne'ohe • Map E4 • 800 735 5071 • www.paradise bayresorthawaii.com • $$

2 Hawai'i's Hidden Hideaway

A short walk from Lanikai and Kailua beaches, these privately owned units are comfortably furnished and well-equipped. All have views of the ocean or the landscaped gardens. ◎ 1369 Mokolea Dr., Kailua • Map F4 • 262 6560 • www.ahawaiibnb.com • $$

3 Ramada Plaza Waikīkī

This 17-story high-rise hotel is at the gateway to Waikīkī and is a short two blocks from the beach. There's a pool and sundeck and a fitness facility; the Chinese Buffet Restaurant offers affordable, bountiful Asian fare. ◎ 1830 Ala Moana Blvd. • Map H6 • 955 1111 • www.ramada. com • $$

4 J & B's Haven

Run by a mother/daughter team, this beautiful house has two comfortable rooms for guests. Floor-to-ceiling windows provide mountain views and two dogs add to the atmosphere. Smoking is not permitted. Breakfast is included. ◎ Kahena St., Hawaii Kai • Map F5 • 396 9462 • www.bb online.com/hi/jbshaven • $$

5 The Breakers Hotel

A 1950s vintage, Hawaiian-style oasis amid towering neighbors, The Breakers prides itself on its Hawaiian-style hospitality. Tropical flowers and a patio surround the pool; there's a kitchenette in every room. And the beach is only a short walk away. ◎ 250 Beach Walk • Map J6 • 923 3181 • www. breakers-hawaii.com • $$

6 Diamond Head Bed & Breakfast

On the side of Kapi'olani Park farthest from Waikīkī, Joanne Trotter has been welcoming guests into her home for over two decades. Her tasteful house with its big *lanai* and tropical gardens is filled with heirlooms and artwork. Breakfast included. ◎ 3240 Noela Drive • Map E6 • 923 3360 • www.diamondheadbnb. com • $$

7 Lanikai Bed & Breakfast

If a comfortable, attractive room in a chic O'ahu area is your cup of tea, this could be the B&B for you. The hosts are warm and knowledgeable; the location across from Lanikai Beach excellent. Each unit has kitchen facilities. ◎ 1277 Mokulua Dr., Kailua • Map F4 • 261 7895 • www.lanikaibeach rentals.com • $$

8 Beach Lane B&B and Cottages

Close to beautiful windward-side beaches and a short drive from activities, these Hawaiian-style accommodations offer a relaxing retreat near Kailua town. Beach supplies are provided. ◎ 111 Hekili St., Box 277, Kailua (mailing address) • Map F4 • 262 8286 • www.beachlane.com • $$

9 Aloha B&B

Comprised of three units with a shared bath in residential – and very upscale – Hawai'i Kai, this affordable B&B has panoramic ocean views. It's a 15-minute drive from Waikīkī and even closer to neighborhood dining and shopping. Rates include continental breakfast. ◎ 909 Kahauloa Place • Map E6 • 395 6694 • www.home.roadrunner. com/~alohaphyllis • $

🔟 Kailua Vacations House of Waterfalls

Four air-conditioned units sit in a lush tropical garden with a solar-heated pool and a waterfall, close to Kailua beach. The units can be rented separately or as one large rental. ◎ 1478 Akialoa Pl., Kailua • Map F4 • 262 7466 • www. kailuavacations.com • $$

General Index

Acknowledgments

The Author
Bonnie Friedman is a freelance writer and publicist living in Hawai'i.

Produced by BLUE ISLAND PUBLISHING

Editors
Michael Ellis, Jane Simmonds, Rosalyn Thiro
Art Director Stephen Bere
Picture Research Ellen Root
Proofreader Val C. Phoenix
Fact Checkers Becky Maltby, Linda Mather Olds
Photographer Nigel Hicks
Additional Photography Andy Crawford, Philip Dowel, David Murray, Ian O'Leary, Rob Reichenfeld, Clive Streeter, Francesca Yorke
Cartography DK India: Managing Editor Aruna Ghose; Senior Cartographer Uma Bhattacharya; Cartographers Suresh Kumar and Alok Pathak

AT DORLING KINDERSLEY

Publishing Manager Helen Townsend
Senior Art Editor Marisa Renzullo
Senior Cartographic Editor Casper Morris
Senior DTP Designer Jason Little
Production Bethan Blase
DK Picture Library Romaine Werblow
Design and Editorial Marta Bescos, Emma Gibbs, Eric Grossman, Laura Jones, Jude Ledger, Nicola Malone, Alison Mcgill, Mary Ormandy, Catherine Palmi, Marianne Petrou, Rada Radojicic, Mani Ramaswamy, Sands Publishing Solutions, Roseen Teare, Conrad van Dyk

Picture Credits
Dorling Kindersley would like to thank all establishments for their assistance.

t=top; tl=top left; tr=top right; c=center; r=right; b=bottom; br=bottom right.

Hockney's Design for Ravel's Opera 'L'Enfant et les Sortileges' 1983, © David Hockney: 65bl; Courtesy of AMPY'S: 54tr, 54bl; ALAMY IMAGES: JTB Photo Communications, inc. 12cla, David L. Moore - oahu 16-17c, Photo Resource Hawaii, Marc Schechter 13clb; ALLAN SEIDEN: 14t, 15t, 15b, 30tl, 30tr, 32tl, 35r, 36tl, 36tr, 36c, 36b, 52c, 96tr, 97t, 97b, 99tr, 99cr, 100tl, 100tr, 101, 104tr; ALOHA STADIUM: 88tc; BISHOP MUSEUM: 10r, 11bc, *Leinihopilimauna* by Marques Marzan 11cb; CHAI'S ISLAND BISTRO: 62tc, 69tl; CORBIS: Bettmann 31tr, 31br, John Hicks 16br;. RON DAHLQUIST: 30b, 32c, 33r, 34tr. PETER FRENCH: 32tr. THE FRIENDS OF IOLANI PALACE: William F Cogswell *Queen Lili'uokalani*, 189115c; © 1992 Milroy/McAleer 14b; HAWAII THEATRE CENTER: David Franzen 67tc; HAWAII TOURISM AUTHORITY (HTA): Ron Garnett 79tl, Tor Johnson 6crb, 16cla; HONOLULU ACADEMY OF ARTS: Gift of the Christensen Fund 2001, *Garuda*, India 17th c. 7tr; Paul Gauguin *Two Nudes on a Tahitian Beach*, 1892 18c; Utagawa Hiroshige *53 Stations of the Tokaido Road, Station 16: Night Snow at Kambara* 18b; Kuan-Yin Bodhidttva, Chinese Northern Sang Dynasty, wood 19t; Theodore Wores *The Lei Maker*, 1902 19c; Courtesy of HOTELS & RESORTS OF HALEKULANI: 58tl; KELKI BEACH BUNGALOWS: 120tl; Courtesy of KO OLINA GOLF COURSE: 37r, 50b. O'AHU VISITORS BUREAU: 17cr; PARADISE BAY RESORT; 121tl; DOUGLAS PEEBLES: 44-5, 52b, 56tl, 56b, 60-1, 77t; Wildlife Images/ Michael Nolan 114tl; PUKA DOG HAWAII: 74tl; Courtesy of RUMOURS NIGHTCLUB: 68tr.
All other images © Dorling Kindersley. For further information see: **www.DKimages.com**

Special Editions of DK Travel Guides

DK Travel Guides can be purchased in bulk quantities at discounted prices for use in promotions or as premiums. We are also able to offer special editions and personalized jackets, corporate imprints, and excerpts from all of our books, tailored specifically to meet your own needs.

To find out more, please contact:
(in the United States) **SpecialSales@dk.com**
(in the UK) **TravelSpecialSales@uk.dk.com**
(in Canada) DK Special Sales at **general@tourmaline.ca**
(in Australia) **business.development @pearson.com.au**

Glossary of Useful Words & Terms

Hawaiian began as an oral language and was put into written form by missionaries who arrived in the 1820s. The teaching and speaking of Hawaiian was banned from the early 1900s, and by the time the native cultural renaissance began in 1978 the melodious language was almost totally lost. Immersion programs are beginning to produce a new generation of Hawaiian speakers, however, and you will hear Hawaiian words sprinkled in conversation and in the islands' music, as well as seeing it written on some signs.

SUMMARY OF PRONUNCIATION

The Hawaiian language has just 12 letters: the five vowels plus h, k, l, m, n, p, and w.

unstressed vowels:

a	as in "above"
e	as in "bet"
i	as y in "city"
o	as in "sole"
u	as in "full"

stressed vowels:

ā	as in "far"
ē	as in "pay"
ī	as in "see"
ō	as in "sole"
ū	as in "moon"

consonants:

h	as in "hat"
k	as in "kick"
l	as in "law"
m	as in "mow"
n	as in "now"
p	as in "pin"
w	as in "win" or "vine"

The 'okina (glottal stop) is found at the beginning of some words beginning with vowels or between vowels. It is pronounced like the sound between the syllables in the English "uh-oh."

ali'i	ahlee-ee
liliko'i	leeleekoh-ee
'ohana	oh-hahnah

The kahakō (macron) is a mark found only above vowels, indicating vowels should be stressed.

kāne	**kah**-nay
kōkua	**koh**-koo-ah
pūpū	**poo**-poo

EVERYDAY WORDS

aloha	ah-loh-ha	hello; goodbye; love
hale	ha-leh	house
hula	who-la	Hawaiian dance
kāhiko	**kaa**-hee-koh	old, traditional
kapa	kah-pah	bark cloth
keiki	kay-kee	child
kōkua	**koh**-koo-ah	help
lānai	**luh**-nigh	porch; balcony
lei	layh	garland
lua	looah	bathroom
mahalo	muh-ha-low	thank you
'ono	oh-noh	delicious
ko'olau	koh-oh-lowh	windward side

GEOGRAPHICAL & NATURE TERMS

'a'ā	ah-**aah**	rough, jagged lava
kai	kaee	ocean
koholā	koh-hoh-**laah**	humpback whale
mauna	mau-nah	mountain
pāhoehoe	**pah**-hoy-hoy	smooth lava
pali	pah-lee	cliff
pu'u	poo-oo	hill
wai	w(v)hy	fresh water

HISTORICAL TERMS

ali'i	ahlee-ee	chief; royalty
heiau	hey-yow	ancient temple
kahuna	kah-hoo-nah	priest; expert
kapu	kah-poo	taboo
kupuna	koo-poo-nah	elders; ancestors
luakini	looah-kee-nee	human sacrifice temple
mana	mah-nah	supernatural power
mele	meh-leh	song
oli	oh-leeh	chant

FOOD WORDS

'ahi	ah-hee	yellowfin tuna
aku	ah-koo	skipjack; bonito
a'u	ah-oo	swordfish; marlin
haupia	how-peeah	coconut pudding
kalo	kah-loh	taro
kālua	**kah**-looah	food baked slowly in an underground oven
laulau	lau-lau	steamed filled ti-leaf packages
liliko'i	lee-lee-koh-ee	passion fruit
limu	lee-moo	seaweed
lomi-lomi salmon	low-me low-me	raw salmon with onion and tomato
lū'au	**loo**-ow	Hawaiian feast
mahimahi	muh-hee-muh-hee	dorado; dolphin fish
poi	poy	pounded taro
pūpū	**poo**-poo	appetizer
uku	oo-koo	gray snapper
ulua	oo-looah	jackfish

PIDGIN

Hawai'i's unofficial conglomerate language is commonly heard on the street and in backyards throughout Hawai'i. You may hear:

brah	brother, pal
broke da mout'	great food
fo' real	really
fo' what	why
grinds	food; also to grind
howzit?	how's everything?
kay den	okay then
laydahs	later; goodbye
no can	cannot
no mo' nahting	nothing
shoots!	yeah!
stink eye	dirty look
talk story	chat; gossip